Dr Lashutka

M000307173

Choosing Life

BEYOND THE BIG C

Thanks for your role in
my healing

Hazel

My Journey Through Cancer

BY HAZEL CHANDLER MA, BS

The material contained in this book is my journey and is provided is for informational purposes only. It is not intended to diagnose, treat or cure any diseases or illnesses. I am a person living with cancer, not a medical professional. I am committed to the decision that I made for my own healing, but make no guarantees about effectiveness for another. Each of us is different, and our journey is different. Therefore the reader is encouraged to search within and determine if the information provided is useful. The statements in this book have not been evaluated by the Food and Drug Administration.

Copyright © Hazel Elaine Chandler 2016

Photo and graphics by M. Jennifer Chandler and Daniele Chandler used with permission.

Dedication

To my children and grandchildren—
the greatest gifts of life:

Richard, Jennifer, Beth, Daniele, Jeff,
Brandon, Eric, Becky, Ryan, Trevor,
Maddie and Benjamin.

To Randy and Sara who have departed
from the realm of this earth, but
continue to guide my life on a minute
by minute basis.

To my Mom, whose transition made
publishing this book possible.

Acknowledgements

Recognizing all the people that helped make this book possible would require a book in itself. All my family, friends, colleagues both past and present have had a huge impact on creating the energy that allowed me to complete this account of my journey through cancer.

I would like to acknowledge and thank my daughter Jennifer (M Jennifer Chandler) whose photos appear throughout the book. She has developed the beautiful cover as well as assisted with this book in so many ways that I cannot even start to list all of them. Jennifer has been my sounding board, editor, creative coach, and she has blessed me with many beautiful photos to choose from. She has listened when I was ready to give up on this book and encouraged me to take a fresh look the next day. Her belief that I could be an author allowed me the courage to move forward.

I would like to also recognize my daughter-in-law Daniele Chandler, who created the graphic for the introduction, and also helped me create many other graphics. An author herself, she was a never-tiring sounding board as I worked through the ideas. She also served as editor, creative coach. Her courage to publish her own book gave me courage for my own.

I also must thank Vickie Brown and Celeste Levesque (my two best friends) for always being there for me.

A special thanks to Dr. Colleen Huber and her staff. They have helped me in the healing process. Dr. Huber in spite of a grueling schedule took time to review this book and give me encouragement along the way. I am so grateful to have found this wonderful clinic. A special thanks to Lori, the first face at the clinic. Her smile lifted my spirits in the darkest hours.

I would also like to thank Liam Quirk of River City eMarketing who has been a friend and my tireless editor. His encouragement has been instrumental moving this book forward.

INTRODUCTION

The lessons contained in this memoir are focused on my journey both **through** and **beyond** cancer. I've learned how essential it is to uncover the root cause of disease, and I am convinced that *all* dis-ease is an opportunity to open up our hearts to the truth of our beings.

Sadly, we are losing the war on cancer because we are searching for a cure outside ourselves rather than finding the root cause within. And make no mistake about it removing the root cause is the only way to win!

So, I invite you to come along on this journey of inner discovery, of finding the root cause within, and of understanding that when we want something our whole life conspires to help us get it.

My greatest hope in sharing my journey is that it will help you along yours, as well.

Hazel Elaine Chandler

Table of Contents

Chapter 1

My Journey

When life puts you in tough situations, don't say, "WHY ME?" Just say, "TRY ME!"

7/11 has been a magical number for me: a symbol that I am embraced in the arms of a creative power greater than my understanding. It is a reminder that each of us is a child of this greater creative force which connects us all.

On 7-11-2012, I received news that changed my life forever. The magical power of this date always reminds me of the greater creative force at work in all things, including the news I was about to receive.

That day when the phone rang, I received a call most of us dread. Our worst nightmare! The nurse practitioner on the other end of the line said, "We have the results of your tests. You have breast cancer." She further explained how serious it was and that I had multiple cancerous lumps. She told me to see an oncologist and a surgeon immediately. After giving me names of surgeons and oncologists she recommended she added a final warning... "This is very serious. You need to get an appointment immediately. Do not delay in getting these appointments."

I took a deep breath, followed by a moment of panic. With the very next breath, I realized I was being given a precious opportunity to take another step towards mastery on the journey of this life.

Faced with the choice of living in fear, of the future, or living in the moment and embracing life's journey, I quickly chose LIFE.

Did I want to take this journey – **NO WAY!** – Was I willing to do the necessary work toward self-understanding and healing – **Absolutely!**

What was magically shown to me by the significance of the date of diagnosis, 7-11, was that a greater power or creative force, greater than myself, was orchestrating this adventure. I was being asked to redefine who I was in the process.

In this moment, I realized, I was **vibrantly healthy** in spite of the test results. The journey began to live in that vibrantly healthy moment as I moved beyond the "Big C."

That day, I knew my journey would require commitment, discipline, and compassion for myself. I needed to trust in the higher power and learn not to let those around me take my power away.

That day, I knew I would not take the journey that most cancer patients take. I'll talk more about my reasons later, but chemo and radiation were not options for me.

I could live my life as a tragedy, or I could embrace a loving and deep journey towards healing. My story would unfold, in my way; I am the scriptwriter and leading actress in my life story... And I really much prefer love stories.

Several years ago, I had the opportunity to get to know Elizabeth Kubler-Ross, often considered one of the foremost experts on death and dying. In talking about healing Elizabeth would say that disease was an opportunity to undertake a healing journey. She would stress that some of us are able to heal to life, but others found their healing during the dying process and actually healed into death.

I am a person strongly committed to living a peaceful life and knew that declaring war on cancer was not in alignment with who I am and my journey through the life plane.

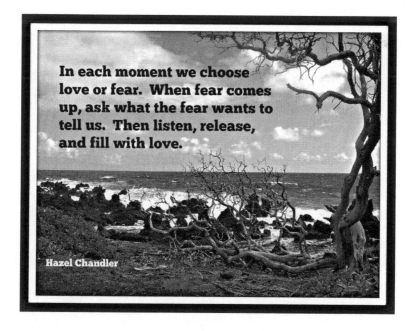

In each moment we choose love or fear. When fear comes up, ask what the fear wants to tell us. Then listen, release, and fill with love.

Hazel Chandler

For me, finding ways to love myself, love the Big C cells in my body and stimulate my immune system would ultimately lead my body to a vibrantly healthy state.

This was not about destroying the Big C cells but retraining them to function in the way that the body intended. The first step was to decide that despite what the medical tests showed – I was in fact vibrantly healthy. In each moment, I could choose again. I could choose to live life fully every single moment or spend my precious moments worrying about the future. I chose to live fully, embrace every single moment and find a support team to support my healing process. I chose to live life, not to use each moment to move one step closer to death.

Most of us struggle to fully live life. Some view that each breath is taking us one moment closer to death. I choose to embrace that with every breath comes a fuller understanding and a much greater embodiment of life. The rat race most of us live in has generated a sub-conscious desire to simply give up on life. For the most part, I thought that I was fully living life, but after extensive self-reflection, I realized a part of me had been giving up on life. That day I committed to fully live *my* life, to show up fully in each moment, experience and embrace what life has to offer.

My journey with the Big C has led to a more vibrantly healthy and engaged life. Maybe the most engaged and in charge that I have ever been. I made an agreement to myself to show up for life with the fullness of myself, not just in the ways that I thought other people wanted me to. Magical things began to happen. Like the words of the serenity prayer, I have come to a greater understanding of the things that I cannot change, developed the courage to confront the things that I can change and gained the ability to discern the difference. This enhanced life force energy has allowed me to fully engage in life with a really challenging schedule.

Transformation
is usually
planted
by seeds
of doubt
that hairpin
curves reveal.
Doubt is one
of the grandest
birthing experiences
in earth school.

Cancer for me was one of the hairpin curves
that allowed me to overcome doubt and fear to
birth a new version of myself, allowing me
to live life more fully and vibrantly.
Hazel Chandler

Through this memoir, my story about life beyond the Big C, I am able to share my journey toward healing. Please know and understand that this is my journey, a precious story of my challenges and discoveries. I welcome you to use my experiences to assist with your own journey with the awareness and knowing that each of us has a unique path and unique lessons to learn. Through time in prayer, meditation and listening to my own body, I discovered my path to moving beyond the Big C. Each of you must do your own soul searching to determine the best course of action for healing yourselves.

For some people facing a cancer diagnosis, the medical route of chemo, surgery and radiation may be the best approach. For others, a combination of the medical treatment with healthy diet, supplements, exercise, meditation, and alternative treatments may be the best route. Heed this caution: if you choose to take your healing process into your own hands, you will be guaranteed to have all of your demons in your face. Whatever you decide, I encourage you to become informed and ask lots of questions. A few days' delay to research and get answers will not have a major impact on the ultimate outcomes.

The idea of cancer is scary, and many of you will encounter people who will not support the decisions that you are making. We have grown accustomed to listening to the advice of doctors, rather than listening to our own bodies. Not only is it daunting to ourselves, but to our families, too.

In fact many people seem to have a harder time supporting someone on the alternative journey than the traditional medical approaches. Be prepared for challenge from within and from the loved ones around you. For instance, when I told my mom who is a breast cancer survivor (she had a nightmare experience but lived an additional 27 years) that I was going the alternative way, she was highly reluctant. She seemed supportive over the phone, but within minutes the phone was ringing off the hook with my aunts and cousins calling trying to talk me into doing chemo and radiation.

My kids were loving and supportive, but shared their fears of the journey that I chose. Even my daughter, Jen, who believes firmly in alternative medicine needed to meet my doctors, see my therapy and ask questions to gain comfort.

Whatever decisions you choose, I support you. I encourage you to remember the tremendous power of healing that we have inside each of us. We were created in the image of GOD and GOD does not make junk. You are very special, a precious addition to our world. You came with a unique blueprint, a sacred contract for your life. Remember that a cancer diagnosis may be your ticket to a greater, more fulfilled life, but you may have to choose deep change in order to choose life. Here's to healing!!!!! Now, go toast to your journey with a vegetable juice.

Chapter 2

What the AIDS Epidemic Taught Me About Life, Death and Healing

EVERY human being is the author of his own health or disease.

Buddha

Photo by M Jennifer Chandler

In the late 80s and early 90s, I had the opportunity to experience many powerful lessons by working with people living with AIDS. As a straight female this seemed like a strange path to take, but through a number of divinely guided twists and turns on my life's path, an amazing journey fell into my lap. The lessons learned through this experience were instrumental in my journey beyond cancer.

I believe that AIDS came to the gay community to help them learn to give and receive love and to teach others how to love. Mostly to be able to love themselves, but also to love others who were judging them as wrong. I am not talking about sexual love

– That is not love. I am talking about the spiritual energy that connects us with our own soul and with each other, soul to soul.

In the late 80s and early 90s many of the incredible gay men who were living with AIDS taught me what love really is. In spite of a life-threatening disease and a world around them judging them and "their" disease as evil, many of these very special souls were able to rise above the judgment. I watched as it led them to a journey of healing. This uncompromising process of life or death impacted those blessed enough to cross paths with their journey in ways beyond words. I witnessed as they learned how to move into a place of complete love, which raised them above judgment of self and others. Many were able to forgive those who had judged them, abused them and even persecuted them. Were any of them able to do this all of the time? Absolutely not, but I watched as they diligently tried.

They were beings having a challenging spiritual journey and learning the tough lessons of life school. Many of these people had childhoods and even adult lives that others would deem nightmarish. Most had histories in early childhood of abuse, substance abuse and addiction in their families of origin. Many had faced society's judgment about their sexual orientation and suffered a seemingly tortured life. Substance abuse, sexual addictions and self-destructive behaviors were the norm amongst many of the people I encountered. In spite of all of this, many individuals were able to rise above and bring healing into their lives and to the lives of those that were privileged to be around them.

The love and community I felt working during the AIDS movement in the late 80s and early 90s was like nothing I had ever experienced before. To this day, I seldom experience real love and community to the same depth as what I experienced during that time of my life. In many ways these experiences prepared me for my journey through and beyond cancer. I steadfastly believe these incredible souls came into this life to help many of us learn some very important lessons. My dream is that sharing my own journey will help others to be able to experience these lessons as well.

Back in the late 80s and early 90s everyone believed that AIDS was 100% fatal. The question was not *if* someone would die, but **when**. This belief system was so strong that many bought into their own fears and into this common cultural belief. This cultural belief system was so strong that few were able to escape the rabbit hole, and most accepted the belief that AIDS was terminal. The ones that maintained the healthiest life were the ones that embraced a holistic approach to treatment. They changed their entire way of life. They allowed the strength within their bodies to provide the energy to heal. For many, they had to accept change in order to choose life.

Many others turned to the medical community and relinquished their power over their own bodies in order find medical help. Over and over people with AIDS became guinea pigs for very toxic medications and treatments. Often their bodies were not strong enough to withstand the onslaught of these toxic cocktails of emerging medications. At that time, I was extremely critical of many of these treatments. What I witnessed was astounding. Vibrant men lost their life force within weeks of starting these treatments. What I realized was that fear was causing them to disconnect from their own life force energy, and their bodies could no longer support life.

I wonder how popular, currently emerging trends would have assisted them in maintaining their life force energy and if alternative methods would have had an effect on negating the toxic side-effects of those treatments. I witnessed many men respond well to things like massage, Reiki and other treatments that assisted with increasing and maintaining the body's energy.

One of these amazing men became my best friend in the whole world, Randy. Some might say he was my soulmate. With the exception of my children, I have never had as strong a relationship with another human being as I did with Randy. He was an amazing teacher and spiritual leader. He helped launch thousands on their spiritual journey, including me. Throughout his own journey with AIDS, he was one of the greatest inspirations in my life and the lives of those around him.

Randy would frequently talk about the misguided belief *that AIDS was fatal*. He thought it was a lie and asked me to keep reminding him about this. After many years of his tireless, selfless service, the disease began to take a toll on his physical body. Fear crept in and he turned to medicine for the answers. The toxic combinations of medications began to degrade his body. I witnessed him grow sicker and sicker. We had a number of conversations about what he felt his role on earth was. He affirmed that he felt led to collapse the belief system that AIDS was a fatal disease.

My last conversation with him took place a few days before his transition. He was designing a restaurant and had worked all day to ensure all of the architectural plans and design elements were in order. He remained active and engaged in his life, despite the virus that was taking control of his body. During this conversation, he reminded me of the unique gifts that each of us holds within us and continued to encourage me to rise above others' beliefs and the prescribed ways in which we live our lives. Randy told me then that he knew AIDS was not fatal, but if he needed to leave to transcend this belief, he would be willing to leave this earth. He reminded me that this life is just a drop in the bucket - insignificant with significance. He felt strongly that coming to terms with that was instrumental in helping others to realize that disease was really an illusion, a reflection of the parts of ourselves where love cannot reside, where we judge ourselves and others.

A few days later, after putting the final touches on several design projects, he began his dying process. I was living many miles away in Texas; he was in Arizona. While in the shower, I got an intuitive message that his end was nearing. After a quick phone call to a friend it was confirmed that he had taken a turn for the worse, and the end was in fact rapidly approaching.

My journey to return to Phoenix is a story in itself -- supported by what I can only describe as divine intervention. Within 45 minutes of the after-shower phone call, I was boarding a plane at Love Field in Dallas. The airport was 35 minutes from my house. I made airline reservations, arranged for a rental car, packed, got to the airport and boarded the plane in less than 45 minutes. I have no explanation. It was after I got on the plane that I realized that I had unconsciously checked my luggage. At the time, Southwest Airlines required passengers of any flights between Dallas and Phoenix to change planes, pick up luggage and recheck it in New Mexico, and typically all flights had to have an hour lay-over.

When my plane landed in New Mexico, I was met at the gate by a staff person from Southwest Airlines. She told me that I was being moved to a flight leaving immediately. I said I needed to get my luggage, and she said not to worry, that they would take care of it. I thought at the time that I really did not care if I ever got my things back – just get me to Phoenix. To this day I think angels played a big role in the change of plane. I landed in Phoenix two hours before I should have. When I ran downstairs, my luggage was sitting next to the luggage carousel waiting for me. The rest of the plane's luggage had not arrived. To this day I have no idea how it or I got there. The rental car agency had the paperwork completed and the car waiting right by the door. I was at Randy's house, a half hour from the airport, still two hours before I should have arrived at the airport. Something was really interesting with how time operated that day.

By 1:00 I was sitting at Randy's bedside and never left his side with the exception of pit stops to the bathroom throughout the day. When I arrived he squeezed my hand so I knew he knew I was there, but he never opened his eyes. To me it was obvious that his soul had /or was moving into another realm.

I was given the tremendous gift of spending most of that time in the other realm with him, receiving incredible teachings about the reality of life and death, and the purpose and meaning of life. I don't remember much, or at least that I could put in words, but I know that my life changed forever. Not just the changed forever feeling of losing someone you love, but a deep level of feeling and knowing I hadn't realized existed. On the second day in the early afternoon, with two other cherished friends and I at his bedside, we thought he had taken his last breath. Simultaneously, as we thought he was drawing his last breath, I saw a vision of all of the friends that had gone before him preparing a party. Lots of chocolate kisses, more balloons than I had ever seen and amazing food – you know, gay guys can really throw a party!! The words came through in my mind, "No! No! You can't come yet—the party does not start until 7:11." A couple of seconds later he took another breath. We continued to sit with him and to have otherworldly experiences and deep sensations of life lessons.

When he took his last breath that evening I looked up from the bed where I was sitting next to his empty body, and across from me the digital clock said 7:11. For the first time in his entire life he arrived exactly on time; he was always notoriously late. The only other time I ever knew him to get anywhere on time was the day he helped me open to my spiritual journey nine years earlier.

For me, it was both interesting and significant that Randy chose to pass at 7:11, as that number was a symbol of spiritually and love that was a secret communicated only between us. To this day most days I see 7:11 as well as other times with 11 minutes on the clock, and it is a reminder that he is always right by my side.

Within a couple of weeks of his transition, I begin to notice the conversation around AIDS was changing. Discussions began to focus on AIDS as a chronic disease that could be managed by treatment, rather than a death sentence. Newly emerging treatment protocols were replacing the toxic ones. And the new drugs of choice used in lower dosages or in conjunction with other drugs that did not have the side effects of the proceeding cocktails Randy and many of the people I knew had used. The major shift was that we were no longer hearing that AIDS was 100% fatal. I would like to think that he and his death played a role in creating this energetic shift.

Is this a lesson for all of us that are dealing with terminal or chronic disease? I think so. I believe that every day the beliefs and fears of society are impacting the roads that we take when we are faced with illness. Are those of us who choose to retain our personal power as we walk through Cancer and other life threatening diseases the ones that will change the belief system around all disease? I think so.

The gay community has made great strides in the last 20 years in accepting themselves and helping society accept their life choices. We now understand that this is a disease not only isolated to sexual orientation or IV drug users, but has affected everyone. New cases of AIDS are rare in the gay community. It has now broadened its reach. Currently we see an emerging epidemic of AIDS in the African American community and young heterosexuals. Are similar early experiences, self-judgment, lack of self-esteem, "not pretty enough" taking its toll in this community as well? We now have many incredible people within the young adult and African American community that are just like those amazing gay men that planted the seeds of teaching others what true love is and how to heal.

Cancer is another opportunity for healing ourselves and others, through the lessons it offers. I believe that cancer reflects what is eating away at our body – illustrating the ways we have disconnected from our body, mind and soul. It is rogue cells going wild. When you look at most people living with cancer, a high percentage have had difficult childhoods, and many have lived challenging lives where their quest to be recognized has kept them from taking care of their own needs and their body. The judgments of ourselves – and the fear of what others will think if we stay true to ourselves – allows the cells to begin to grow out of control.

The unlived life within us is crying to be lived. When the hamster wheel of life gets too much to handle, at a deep soul level we are giving up on life. One of the things that I realized about myself after my diagnosis was that I was showing up in life, but particularly at work, with only part of myself. Through deep introspection I discovered that this was actually true of every aspect of my life. I had fears that if people really saw me that I would be rejected. An appropriate diagnosis might be the *disease to please*. Research tells us that many women with Breast Cancer have the disease to please. Those skills date back to my childhood. Being the oldest child, I always was trying to please everyone. My relationship with my younger sister could sometimes be difficult, and at times aggressive. In times when things got heated between us and I fought back, I was always the one who got in trouble with my parents.

I was also on the forefront of women's liberation, and often was in leadership roles that had previously only been occupied by men. I have always felt that I had to work many times harder than a man would. If I took time to take care of myself, others would not approve and perhaps would try to overthrow my authority. Heaven forbid if I took an extra hour off or played hooky from work. I always worked way more than the 40 hours required, and most of the time felt that I was not doing enough. I set very high expectations of myself and what I was supposed to be able to accomplish.

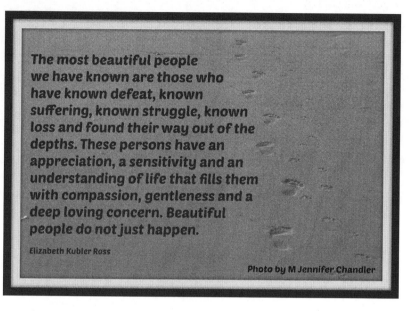

The most beautiful people we have known are those who have known defeat, known suffering, known struggle, known loss and found their way out of the depths. These persons have an appreciation, a sensitivity and an understanding of life that fills them with compassion, gentleness and a deep loving concern. Beautiful people do not just happen.

Elizabeth Kubler Ross

Photo by M Jennifer Chandler

My journey through healing has required me to take a deep look at those issues. I have come to realize that I have a choice to let all of that self-doubt and self-criticism go -- and move into a new place of accepting myself. I am an incredible spiritual being – Just like you - having a human experience. In that human experience everything that I have done, every twist and turn my life path has taken was for a reason to help me move more deeply and comfortably into who I really am.

Chapter 3

The Unlived Life

The day which we fear as our last is but the birthday of eternity."

-Lucius Annaeus Seneca-

Wthat I have come to understand reflecting back on the journey working with AIDS and other terminal illnesses and the twists and turns that my journey has taken, is that there was an unlived life within me that was almost like a bomb ready to explode. I had spent my life building others' dreams, and my greatest dreams were caught in the prison of inner space inside of me. Most of us have an unlived life within us. Some of these amazing people that I worked with, that were living with AIDS, for the first time were able to live the unlived life within them. Even if it was for a short period of time, many times with the body breaking down, many were able to live the life of their dreams.

Elizabeth Kubler Ross once told me that we have opportunities to heal back into life or heal through our process of letting go of the body.

I am thinking that we could take that one step further. AIDS, Cancer, Immune Disorders, Chronic illness allows us the opportunity to reevaluate our lives and maybe open doors for us to begin to live that unlived life. Then we have the opportunity to determine if we want to renew our contract and continue in the life plane or not to renew and easily shed our body.

I heard someone talk the other day about death as returning the rental car on empty. For the short time that we are on earth our bodies are like a rental car to carry our soul through life. When all of that life force is expended the rental car is returned. I totally believe from my personal near-death experience and the journey I have taken with many people while making their transition, that death is really just graduation to another realm. Really it is just returning the rental car.

I am 100% confident that life goes on. I had many of my friends that knew they were dying purposely set up intentional messages they would send to me to confirm that life goes on after death. Every single person sent the message not once, but many times. Some days when I am really in the flow I get messages from many of these wonderful souls, and I feel their love and support on my continued journey through life.

When people can look at life in this way, it has been my experience that when people can look at life in this way, when they then reach the point that they need to leave this live, they do so easily and gracefully. We come to earth school with a contract that we are to fulfill, a gift that we are to give the earth, and when that contract is fulfilled we have the opportunity to renegotiate another contract or move on to another realm.

When we stay on life's hamster wheel and ignore the inner callings toward the life that we are destined to live is when disease sets in. Environmental issues, and the ways that we do not honor our body temple definitely have an impact, but when we deny ourselves in any way we set up the environment for disease.

Denying self is a slow suicide. Instead of living we are actually dying life. Each of us chooses in each moment to live life or slowly die life. In my experience those that choose to continue to deny self will have the most difficult journey to death, often suffering for many years.

From my work with people with AIDS and other terminal illnesses, I realized that there is never a stage of the disease that cannot be turned around. Over and over I saw people on their death beds that recovered completely.

We are constantly changing. There is never a stage of disease that cannot be turned around.

Hazel Chandler
www.beyondthebige.com

Photo by M Jennifer Chandler©

One example is a man I will call Dave. I had the opportunity to share his dying process, and today over 25 years later he is vibrantly healthy. One afternoon we got a call from the hospital saying that they had a man in the final stages of dying. But his significant other was insisting that his wish was to be at Shanti surrounded by people that loved him. The nurse on the phone said he was already in the dying breath and they did not think that he would survive the ambulance ride – literally a block away.

We quickly mustered volunteers to great him when he arrived. Among the small group of people were Reiki masters and others skilled in supporting the energies that allow people to either heal fully or to leave with ease and grace. We sat gathered in a circle with his life partner (who was the only family available as his parents disowned him for being gay). We held hands in meditation without a word for several hours. I was in a deep state of meditation when I saw him leaving the body. I asked quietly in my mind to travel with him so that he would feel supported. Gay men seldom feel supported in life, so I felt it was really important to be there and support him in this way.

I saw him greeted by spiritual energy-beings and some love ones. While I continued to hold his hand in my mind, he was embraced and surrounded with a powerful light. He was told that he needed to return and that he would heal completely and live a long life helping others accept themselves.

About that time I heard others in the room say he was gone, but I stayed with him in the other world. What seemed to be a long time later – probably a couple of minutes – I heard people say he's back. I told the group that I needed to leave, but he would be okay.

The next morning when I arrived at the center he was up walking the halls. Mind you, he weighed less than 85 pounds, was skin and bones, and had not been out of bed for several weeks. A few days later he thanked me for walking with him to the other side and supporting him through the process. He saw and shared what I saw. He knew I was there with him. I had not shared what

I had experienced with any one, so the only way he would have known is if he had been with me.

He got a new contract and fully recovered to live a vibrant life. The last time I saw him he was vibrantly healthy. He was living a life supported by good nutrition, supplements and an active life with no medication. He worked full-time and did a lot to help others live happy vibrant lives. He had even mended fences with his family.

Chapter 4

Facing Life's Dragons – Judgment, Self-doubt

Photo by
M Jennifer Chandler

Train
your mind to see
the beauty in everything. Hazel Chandler

All judgment of others is judging ourselves. Those that judge the most, people that are racist, anti-gay etc., are the most judging of themselves. In truth every one of us judges at some time. Most of us judge as our everyday way of life. As we begin to become more aware of our thoughts we begin to fully understand how often we judge others and look carefully at the ways we are also judging ourselves.

All addictions, terrorism, and violence root in judging self and fears gone wild.

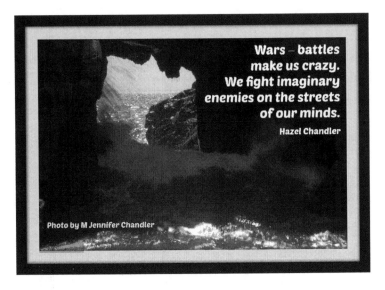

Wars – battles make us crazy. We fight imaginary enemies on the streets of our minds.

Hazel Chandler

Photo by M Jennifer Chandler

When we send our young men to war we expect them to kill or be killed. In fact in many cases even if they survive battle we have killed their soul.

Just like the young men that we send to war, addictions, terrorism, violence, self-judging and fears on the inner battle field are killing our souls. Many have unthinkable childhood experiences that have programed their brains for fear and judgment. Others are programed daily through the media and video games. When is enough, enough?

All judgment is rooted in fear. Fear is the soul trying to communicate. Fear is separation from the whole. As I have walked the spiritual path I have come to realize that there are really only two emotions- **Love or Fear**. In each moment we can choose love or fear. I feel strongly that when we chose love we turn on a healing switch within our bodies that can assist in turning off the rogue cells that we call cancer.

How can we find that healing switch? I believe it lies buried deeply within our inner space. In an age where space travel is commonplace, I believe that journey into our inner space is crucial in moving beyond disease in our bodies and on our planet. How do we journey into our inner space? This I believe is deeply personal and unique for everyone, but I can share some of the tools that I have used that have moved me closer to who I really am and a life beyond the "Big C." I believe the secret to healing is a four letter word – **LOVE**. Not the media definition of love, but a definition that can only be defined within our heart.

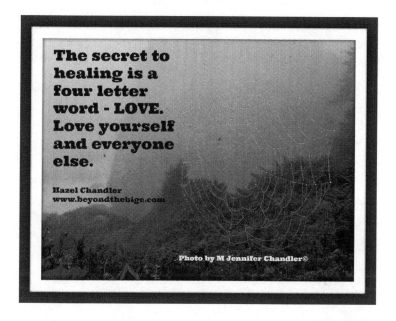

The secret to healing is a four letter word - LOVE. Love yourself and everyone else.

Hazel Chandler
www.beyondthebigc.com

Photo by M Jennifer Chandler©

One of the most important things for me on this journey has been meditation, stillness, and living life in the moment. Again living in the moment was a huge gift that my friends with AIDS helped me understand at a very deep level. We can transcend layers of resistance through meditation, stillness, staying in the now, but the most important is to keep our feet moving towards our dreams.

Meditation is a daily practice. This practice looks different for each person. For some, meditation can be a prayer practice. All I can say is that staying dedicated to a meditation practice has had an amazing impact on my life and my ability to look deeply within my inner space. After years of practice, I have found that my life is now the meditation. Am I in that meditation all of the time? – No way, but for the most part it just takes over and brings a level of peace and happiness that I have never felt before the meditation practice.

Remember when I was first diagnosed with the "Big C," and I took a couple of breaths and was able to understand that there was a greater purpose to the journey that I was about to take? If you are just diagnosed and have never meditated, I encourage you to check it out. Whatever the course of treatment that you choose, I feel that meditation can be a big help.

Research shows that people that meditate while waiting to be wheeled into the operating room for surgery have better outcomes and faster healing. Many people report that meditation during chemo/radiation treatments assist in mitigating the side effects. Check in and see what you inner guidance tells you, and follow that guidance. I believe a big step in the healing process is to learn what your body trying to tell you.

When we enter the inner journey and the deeper we dig, the more dragons begin to come to the surface. Every one of us has tremendous storehouse of dragons buried within our inner space. Some of this is from experiences within our life, possibly past lives and generational memory buried within our DNA, and maybe even Karma of the earth itself.

When we are willing to face our dragons, the dragons lose their power to impact our lives. Our dragons have been our internal inmates. Do we make friends with those dragons, or do we continue to fight the dragons? I believe that it is everyone's question who is on the path to healing. For some, those dragons are so painful that we do everything to avoid facing them, but sooner or later we can no longer keep them hidden and stay on the earth plane. It just gets to painful. The dragons that we refuse to face or continue to fight are the ones that show up in our bodies as rogue cells growing out of control. To heal we must face and make friends with those dragons. These dragons are the life lessons that have been set up for us to have to the tools necessary to fulfill our sacred contract.

If those dragons are too painful to face by yourself, I encourage you to seek out a therapist that has the special skills in helping un-root those dragons. I caution that you need to be extremely careful in choosing a therapist, as many seem to be most skilled in keeping you trapped in battle with the dragons. Make sure they are able to help you recognize the gifts that the dragons have given you and allow you to open the locks of the prison that have held these dragons so securely within your inner space.

For me it was very important to do this inner work without any medications, drugs or alcohol. These substances in my experience only numb us to the pain of our demons, and using them only locks the dragons away deeper in the inner prison cells with tighter and tighter locks. When we have the courage to really feel the pain, the magical key goes in the lock and releases the dragons.

I love the children's movie "How to Train a Dragon." A young Viking boy named Hiccup does not seem to fit into the tribal rituals of slaying dragons. The immense pressure from the tribe to slay dragons weighs heavily on the boy's mind. Through it all he stands firm that he cannot kill a dragon. Through many twists and turns he befriends the most powerful dragon—who has been injured. After overcoming an initial fear, he finds a way to help the dragon build an extension on a wing that allows the dragon again to fly. Through the two movies, the friendship between the two grows, while the criticism of family and friends grows as well. This includes rejection from his father the leader. Finally when the village is threatened by outward forces the boy and his dragon friends come to the rescue and save the village.

The entire village eventually embraces the dragons, and they live happily together supporting each other in many ways. This story illustrates that as we begin to make friends with our inner dragons we find they bring us better understanding of life itself and allow us to move to greater and greater levels of peace, happiness and security.

Cancer itself is not a dragon, but a reflection of the toll that the dragons are having within our inner being. As we begin to make friends with those dragons (a metaphor for fear), we can begin the true healing process. Just like Hiccup, I cannot kill my dragons. To stay true to my soul I must make friends with them and understand the lessons that they have come to tell me.

I believe every experience in life has a reason and is an opportunity to move our soul journey and that of planet earth forward. Every choice that we make, every interaction, every breath, every step has an impact on the greater whole that we call earth. Making peace with our own dragons opens up a space for others to follow. One thought, one action at a time we begin the healing process for our body, and through that healing of ourselves I believe we begin to heal the planet as a whole. I believe real healing occurs when we realize that we are all part of a single organism, and each of us is part of the healing team not only for our own bodies, but the earth and all civilization.

Until we can see the planet as a single organism we will continue to struggle with personal disease and disease as a planet. I used to talk about Planet Earth having AIDS. While I still think that is true, I also think planet earth has Cancer. Those rogue cells in the body of the earth are you and I when we are not living in balance with our true self, not living an authentic life. Healing requires restoring balance within our system. Nature also requires balance to sustain our natural environment, which supports balance, peace and health.

Chapter 5

Smile: You Are On Cosmic Camera

Michael Stamura's quote "Smile you are on Cosmic Camera" is one that really spoke to me. I think it is a great lesson for how to live our lives. When we remember that our lives are constantly being photographed with a Cosmic Camera, it becomes more and more difficult to expend our energy hiding our secrets. I think our energy should be focused on really showing up in our fullness and living life. Here are some of the things that I have realized.

Have fun, play a lot, dance, sing, move – but most of all laugh. Play with the energy and invite it into your body. Dance under the stars and in the first morning light.

One of the greatest thieves of your natural humor and laughter are your secrets. We pretend we can hide things and think no one will know. In fact we're all on Cosmic Camera 24/7. I think it is really interesting in the day of social media how the truth is coming out. The secrets can no longer remain hidden.

If you don't realize this now, you will realize it when you die. I know; I have had a near death experience, and one of the strongest memories was the life review. When I had the opportunity to walk over with others, I was privileged to see their life reviews. Being young, when my near death experience happened, most of my life review was pretty painless. I had lived a pretty clean life. The challenges of life were yet to come. I believe at the core of my being that you will experience the all-seeing, all knowing camera. In my experience this movie of our life was in no way judgmental or critical, but just a review of the lessons of the earth journey.

Hiding things takes an enormous amount of energy, which drains our energy batteries. What if the energy it takes to try to keep these secrets hidden takes the life force energy from our body? What if this is what allows disease to set in? This is a question each of us needs to ask ourselves, but for me this seems to ring true. What I have determined for myself is that the more I can be open and honest about all aspects of my life, the more I feel free-flowing life force energy within. When I try to hide something, I feel that energy jams up within my body.

We can build ways to keep others out, or realize that everything is known so there is no need to keep them inside.

As Tamura said in "You are the Answer," other people's secrets are probably about as interesting as their vacation slides.

As I walked the journey through cancer and worked through the scary process of writing this book, I found that the more honest I became with myself and everyone around me, the stronger the life force energy I felt within my body. My life had been an amazing journey rich in amazing experiences. Even so, a few secrets were holding me hostage in the fear that someone would discover and judge me. I realized the more I could stop judging myself and share some of those life experiences the more my life seemed to flow. In spite of a strong commitment to fully embrace life, to explore what life had to offer, in many ways I have taken life too seriously.

Practice for the next month to have more fun - to play more. Practice each day. Move your body, dance to the energy of music or even the universe. Get quiet and centered and begin to dance to the music of the universe. It takes a little while, but after a little patience the music takes over the body and allows us to dance the dance of the vibration of the universe. This is easier when you are barefoot in nature, but it can also work great right in your front yard or living room floor. I live in a condo with a wonderful lady in the downstairs condo, so I need to be a little careful with dancing on the living room floor. If she is home, I can always invite her to come up to dance with me.

One of the most fun opportunities to play that I have ever had was part of a workshop that I helped organize. We had a number of activities that allowed free form dancing to the energy of the music. We danced to really feel the beat of tribal drums and the flow of ethereal flute music. We also had an exercise to act as silly as possible. If cell phones would have been around in those days, this would have been a great opportunity for selfies or You-tube videos that I am sure would have gotten hits from all over the world. We were laughing hysterically without any thoughts of what anyone else would think.

Next the group of adults had a two hour pre-school experience. We had a dress up corner with ball gowns, tuxes, great hats, boas, make-believe food and real tea served in a tiny tea pots and china cups. The next center was water play, with lots of bowls, pitchers, strainers and squirty toys. How about a little finger painting with chocolate pudding or painting on an Easel with the brightest of colors? The Block corner allowed building the cities of our dreams. I never laughed so hard in my life. Everyone had a ball – by the end everyone came together in a large circle and moved to the rhythm of the universe. The process of the forming the circle was organic. No one said that pre-school was over, it just happened.

It felt like we were under water floating, swaying like seaweed. The sense of the cosmic love was so strong that everyone was rejuvenated and felt they had a new lease on life. Most of all the deep soul connections of the group made us feel like there was only one of us there.

What if we set time on a regular basis to play as a family, as a community, with ourselves or with friends? I am really fortunate to have family and friends that I can do that with, but it happens way too seldom. I believe we are being asked in integrate this into our everyday life – in all of our interactions with people.

Chapter 6

Broken Open – Life's Journey Through Cancer

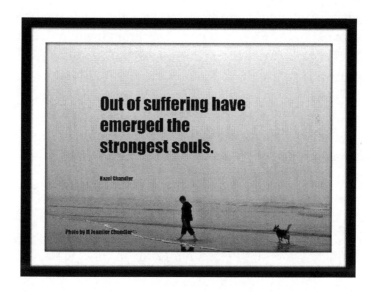

Out of suffering have emerged the strongest souls.

Hazel Chandler

Photo by M Jennifer Chandler©

Τhe diagnosis of cancer is an opportunity to be "Broken Open" to accelerate the exploration of the inner space. For me, I was given a great opportunity to face those internal dragons. It was time to look at all of the ways that I was depleting my life force and the ways I was not fully embracing my dreams and fully showing up for life.

For me I was being asked to give up what no longer works in order to stay close to what is sacred. The priority in my healing was to examine the things in my life that no longer worked or really mattered. It was an opportunity to release old patterns and clutter in my internal and external life. It has also given me an opportunity to have a two-way conversation with the sacred.

Many talk about a Cancer Journey as a deepening of prayer and relationship with God. God is a very personal thing, therefore I choose to call it the sacred, but in fact it is forming a daily, minute-by-minute relationship with God.

It was also a great opportunity to be completely present to what is in front of me. It has allowed me to embrace feelings and thoughts to allow them the freedom from their inner prison. As I bring my thoughts and feelings forward, they have the freedom to move out of my body and no longer drain my internal energy batteries. Remember that each of us has powers that we cannot even imagine. We all have the opportunity to do the work. The key is the willingness to do so. My ego keeps rising up and trying to tell me that I have special powers. In truth my ego is totally wrong; every person on earth has powers within that we cannot even imagine. You and I have exactly the same powers.

Meet the Cancer – Stay in conversation with it – Let it pass through. I am sure that **Resistance** was a big factor in cancer growing within my body. Staying in conversation with the cancer and with my fears has been a big factor in moving beyond the cancer.

Several processes have played a huge role in my healing process, and I would like to share them with you. Each of these processes will become its own chapter..

1. Life inventory
2. Consider options
3. Stay in my own power
4. Make friends with my shadows and fears
5. Create my day
6. Honor my body temple
7. Be impeccable with your words
8. Raise the vibration of your body
9. Relax into the flow of the universe

Chapter 7

Life inventory

Most of our obstacles would melt away if, instead of cowering before them, we should make up our minds to walk boldly through them.

Orison Swett Morden

One of the first steps for me in my healing journey was to conduct an extensive life inventory. I believe that **Life** is a dot-to-dot. The key is to connect the dots and look at the pictures that connects those dots. This I believe is the key to finding the divine within our lives.

Taking a life inventory requires us to really take a look at everything that has impacted our life and set up the opportunity for disease to come into our body. You can develop your own questions, but these are some of the questions that I have used. I took several pads of sticky notes, and for a number of days I pondered these questions. I kept pens and sticky notes everywhere, so if a thought came in, I could record it immediately. I had stacks of random thoughts. I looked at the roles that I had played, people in my life, my belief systems. The key for me was to let the random thoughts flow freely. Many things came up that I did not consciously realize were still impacting my life.

I then took a day. Make sure that you have a quiet place with a full day to be without interruptions. If others live in your house it might be worthwhile to get a hotel (a cabin in the woods would be even better) for the day. I went into meditation and asked that I be able to organize these random thoughts to better understand the patterns that have been running my life. I grouped the thoughts into themes and then started making a pattern on the floor. You could use chart paper, but I just used the floor. I spent several hours grouping these thoughts and making lists of the patterns shown by the reflections of my life patterns that these sticky notes laid out. At the end I chose the things that I wanted to keep and did a ceremony to release those that no longer served. Some of the questions that I looked at were:

What patterns have I experienced in my life that have led me to this place?

What jobs and life experience have led me to this moment?

Who are the people in my life, and how have they impacted my life up to now?

How do the interaction/intersections between these experiences help to reveal my dreams?

After you have completed the inventory and looked at the interactions between all of the life experiences, I encourage you to ponder some of these deep questions.

In several other sessions I pondered questions and more questions. Understanding who we are and finding ways to move beyond these patterns requires us to ask ourselves the right type of questions. These questions should be carefully constructed to dig into the depths of our inner space to help us uproot our greatest fears and greatest desires. Here are some of the questions that I used. I encourage you to ask your soul to help you ask the questions that would be in your highest to ask.

- How do I bring this to the surface to heal and move into my next vibrant inspired role?
- What am I afraid of?
- What does my soul want?
- What does my body want?
- What does my mind want?
- What do I really want?
- What am I most afraid of?
- What would I do, if money was not a factor?
- What would I do, if I knew that every step I take is supported by the universe?
- What is my real job here? What does my Divine Contract say?
- Where are the roots of my patterns of self-sabotage?
- What do I need to do to walk my highest life path every day?
- How can I recognize the chance meeting with a stranger that changes my life to my benefit?
- How do I fully embrace the journey and not the destination?

Remember to have fun; healing needs to include play. An inventory can be difficult, but if you turn it into play – it becomes easier.

Chapter 8

Consider Your Options

We can choose to live life fully in every moment.

Hazel Chandler

Photo by M Jennifer Chandler

very person deserves to be able to make choices that are
aligned with their soul when choosing treatment protocols for serious and life-threatening illness. With the current medical system, many people with cancer feel that the only
choices are toxic; the life-debilitating, so-called "evidence based"
options. While surgery, chemotherapy and radiation assist some
to recover from cancer, my personal experience has been that the
journey through treatments is extremely challenging, not only
requiring many months of suffering and diminished quality of

life, but many times it takes away the person's life force until they give up on life.

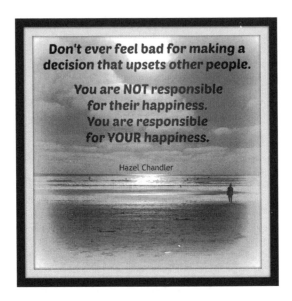

The physicians tell people that there are no other choices if they want to live. Luckily, based on my past experience with family and friends with cancer, I immediately questioned the recommended treatment protocols.

While I was very fortunate to immediately find "Nature Works Best," a naturopathic clinic, most people are unaware that they have a choice. Nature Works Best has the best results of any Cancer Clinic over the last six years. Over and over people are able to heal without toxic options. They also have amazing results with patients that the medical community has given up on. Over and over again I watched stage four cancer patients, whose own medical doctors have told them that there was no hope of recovery, recover with the great treatment provided by Nature Works Best Clinic and return to Vibrant Health. www.natureworksbest.com

For many that are fortunate to find this clinic or a similar clinic, the cost of treatment prevents them from being able to pursue this option. I was really fortunate to be able to pull money from my retirement accounts that allowed me to begin the treatment. After about six months I changed to a progressive insurance company that paid for part of the treatment costs. I am one of the fortunate ones. Over and over, I met people who wanted to pursue this treatment protocol, but could not come up with the funds to move forward.

The cost of traditional cancer treatment protocols can amass huge medical bills. Treatment costs for cancer often run $500,000-$1,000,000 per year, and often require several years of treatment. A single Chemotherapy session can cost $50,000. My two-year treatment from Nature Works Best has cost significantly less than a single bag of Chemo.

In spite of the cost savings of alternative treatment, insurance companies are often unwilling to pay for treatment. Cancer is big business, and tremendous pressure is placed on the medical field to follow the so-called evidence-based medicine. My experience with working in pharmaceutical research leaves me really skeptical of the quality of much of the research. Money plays a big role, and often some of the treatments are pushed into the market without long term studies of impacts the treatments have on long term health.

About a month ago I flew to Portland to attend a "Celebration of Life" for one of my closest, long term friends who made her transition from life after undergoing treatment for Lung Cancer.

This incredible friend had been instrumental in launching my spiritual journey and assisting me to find joy in the simple things in life. We had many adventures together, chasing rainbows, enjoying the beauty of the sunsets and raising our children (who were the best of friends as well). With both of us being single parents, we shared many meals and had many opportunities to serve as a support parent to each other's children.

When she was first diagnosed, she inquired about the treatments that I had used. These treatments were not readily available in Portland, and she did not have the financial resources to pay for the treatments. She felt that she had no choice but to undergo surgery and chemo. Seven months after her diagnosis she took her last breath. During the journey she experienced excruciating pain and spent many days hospitalized. I believe in the end she gave up on life. The pain was too much to bear.

My decision to not do the traditional medical protocol was based on my parents' journeys with cancer. It also was based on the training I received from the National Institute of Health to be a Director for Community Based AIDS research center. First I will talk about my parents' stories.

When my mother was about the age that I was when I was diagnosed, she also received the dreaded diagnosis. She had her mammogram and everything seemed normal, but less than two months later she discovered a lump in her breast. She immediately went through a radical mastectomy, and weeks of chemotherapy. The first series of chemo took its toll. She lost her hair, her immune system was greatly compromised, and she had to curtail her work and social activities significantly. She had relentless nausea, no energy and many other side effects.

A few weeks after the first round of chemo, a large lump was found on the breast wall under the breast that was removed. At the time the only option seemed to be a highly toxic experimental chemotherapy drugs and radiation treatment. After several months of treatment, I received a call that my mom's blood count had fallen so low that they did not feel she was going to make it. It was a few days before Christmas, and the doctors said they did not think she would make it through the weekend, let alone to Christmas. I went to Oregon (home) immediately and found my mother a shell of her former self, barely hanging onto life.

I think having her whole family around her brought life force back into her body, and she was able to survive. I like to think we received a miracle for Christmas. I can sure tell you that a lot of us were having conversations with God. Chemo was stopped, and she was given a short time to recover her strength. She then had a series of radiation.

She was able to recover and passed in October of 2015, living life fully until almost 92. Even so she had long-term issues as a result of the treatment.

A few years ago she was in great pain. She went through many weeks of suffering and tests. Eventually her doctor suspected that she had bone cancer. They finally determined through more test that she had a broken breast bone without experiencing any trauma. They suspected that she had just moved, and it had broken.

She was referred to Walla Walla, WA to the clinic that had treated her previous cancer. Luckily by some miracle, she got one of her original breast cancer doctors. The additional tests that had been completed left this doctor perplexed, so he really starting digging deeper. He came into the appointment with the original records. He realized that the problem area was the bull's eye of the radiation treatment she had received almost twenty years before. The bone structure had been so damaged by the radiation that it had broken with routine movement. She did not have bone cancer, just a bone so weakened that it broke just through everyday movement of the body.

Even though I am really grateful that I have had my mother for over 25 additional years, I would have loved to celebrate her hundredth birthday. She lived her life her way, and when she could no longer live independently slipped out easily without struggle.

She was a really strong woman, and even though I believe I share her strength, I have no desire to go through her journey.

A few years later my father was diagnosed with lymphoma. He also went through the treatment protocols that the doctors recommended. The chemo took its toll on his health, but really did not have much effect on the cancer itself. With his doctor's approval, he stopped treatment. My parents had a great vacation at the Oregon Coast, but his strength never returned. My strong and previously healthy father did not have the strength to bring their 5th wheel back from the coast. My brother had to go get them. When he got home, he gave up on life. In spite of the doctors saying he had at least a year to live, he was gone a few days later. I believe he just gave up on life. The treatment was just too painful.

During the time that I was working with people with AIDS, we applied to the National Institute of Health and were selected to become one of the first Community Based Treatment Facilities approved to do AIDS Research. Over a two year period I traveled to Washington D.C. to train to do AIDS Research with the National Institute of Health. We spent three-four days every six weeks in training and development of research protocols. Most of the participants were doctors, many former cancer doctors, who had moved to treating AIDS or were also treating cancer patients.

Over and over I listened to these doctors argue over how close they could take people to death with the treatment. They all had opinions around how low the blood counts could be taken by the chemo drugs without killing the patients. This confirmed what I already knew: that chemo kills. In some way chemo is playing Russian roulette with the patient's life. I realized that many people actually die of the treatment.

I became very concerned about the integrity of treatments when a treatment was pushed onto us that was a preventive protocol, but the placebo had serious side effects. This preventive protocol was for something that was not a problem in Arizona, but if we moved forward with the community-based site we would have to participate. I began wondering if there might be another option that could enhance life, not deplete the life force.

About that time one of the doctors whom I met at the National Institute of Health left to open an alternative clinic. He was treating AIDS and cancer with IV high-dose Vitamin C and Glutathione and was having some amazing results. At that time I knew that if I was faced with Cancer, I would look into similar options. Over several years his results were so promising that extreme pressure was put on him by his former employer. Eventually he had to close the clinic, but he has continued to conduct leading edge research for alternative and integrative care options.

These experiences and many others led me on a journey to explore alternative and integrative health care. This was such a blessing when I was faced with my own diagnosis, as I have a full tool kit of knowledge about potential treatments to choose from.

Chapter 9

Stay in Your Own Power

Your mind is a
POWERFUL
thing.

Photo by
M Jennifer Chandler

When you fill it with positive thoughts,
your life will start to change.   *Hazel Chandler*

S taying in my own power and making critical decisions for myself was essential in my journey to health. Conventional treatment for Cancer usually takes a patient's power away. The doctors or a treatment team make all of the decisions for most patients, often without even listening to the patient's ideas or wishes. Many patients go into very toxic treatment without fully understanding the potential side effects, long-term health implications or even the truth about the effectiveness of the treatment. Many of these patients lose the ability to listen to the intuitive wisdom of the body, if they ever had that awareness in the first place.

If this is not enough to fully drain a person's power, the insurance companies finish the job. Often medical decisions are made based on what the insurance company will pay for.

For many people, the negotiations with the insurance company is a full-time job. This adds to the stress of the treatments. Many people lose their jobs as a result of the toll the treatments take on the body, further complicating stress, financial burdens and helplessness.

One the things that I have learned through the twists and turns in my life is that to maintain my life force energy, authentic power is critical. This is not a power over others, but a power with each other that feeds the soul. I believe all of us have an unlimited life energy that can flow through our bodies. But experiences, emotions and toxins can block that energy from flowing freely. We develop energy blocks, and after a while these energy blocks can turn into tumors and other cancerous growths. Finding our authentic power allows energy to begin to flow easily through our body and begin the healing process.

Gary Zukav in the great book "Seat of the Soul" defines authentic power as the alignment of the personality with the soul, the harmony, cooperation, sharing and reverence for life. Characteristic of an authentically empowered personality are humility, clarity, forgiveness and love. This has precisely been the journey that I have embarked on.

I have tried to focus my healing journey on maintaining and expanding my authentic power every day. Am I always successful? No way!!! The pain, surfacing fears, work and medical stress often block that authentic power temporarily, but one deep breath and a little centering give me the opportunity to choose again. The more I practice, the easier it gets.

Taking time to play, spend time in nature and with people that I love is a great way to recharge that life force energy and move more fully into my authentic power. Bringing that into your life is a journey, your life journey. Becoming more aware of how we give away our power is the first step in reigniting the life force and bringing that authentic power into our lives. Give it a try. I really recommend reading Gary Zukav's book. It helped me a lot in understanding the process.

Chapter 10

Make Friends With Your Shadows and Fears

TI**he shadow is within all of us, and most of us try to run from it. The shadow is parts of ourselves that we try to deny or even disown. They are the part that yells at our children and does not take responsibility for our actions – the parts that are triggered by life's events.

What I have found is that *the more I try to deny those parts of myself that I do not like or try to stuff my fears and feeling, the more experiences I create that allow these parts and feelings to come to the surface.*

I believe that part of the healing process is to bring those disowned parts of the self to the surface to love and find ways of embracing all of those parts. When we really bring these to the surface and try to understand the messages they have to give us, we have the opportunity to heal this aspect once and for all.

For me, I believe that the pains within the body are often those disowned parts of the self that are crying for recognition. Sometimes in our busy life it is difficult to immediately ask what that pain is trying to tell us, but when I take the time it often disappears.

For those of us that have been on the spiritual journey for a long time, we have been taught to incorporate positive affirmations in our daily life. The tendency with this practice is to only look at what we call positive and continue to bury deeper within inner space the hurts and pains of life. While I really believe that affirmations are critical to creating a life we want to life, giving those other parts of the self a voice is just as important.

I realized in my deep journey into inner space that I wanted other people to embrace their wholeness and greatness, but that I was sabotaging my own. I was afraid that if I showed up with the full me, I would not fit in at my job. I continued to only bring part of me there, and all too often the not-so nice parts seemed to take over.

I hid the parts of me I did not like in the closet. Anger, sadness, loneliness, judgment were buried deep, and I tried my best to keep a happy face, be a nice person, a loving person. These disenfranchised parts of myself kept popping up.

Debbie Ford talks about the Shadow in the great book and movie called "The Shadow Effect." She says that each part of our self is like a beach ball. The more we try to hold the beach balls under the water, the more they want to come up. It is impossible to keep them all under. The beach balls represent the parts of our self that we try to suppress. Any part of our self that we try to suppress keeps popping up until we recognize and embrace those parts.

A number of years ago I had a couple of crying jags where every day for a month or more I would be at the verge of tears for most of the day. I would hold together to go through the work day, but I would get in the car, turn on the ignition and become a blubbering idiot. I am one that goes to incredible lengths to hide sadness, grief, anger and hurt. You get the picture – not very pretty when it all pops out.

After one such crying jog that lasted for over 30 days, I thought I would be smart and ask the universe to help me release those emotions through my nose – Probably not a good idea – I had a runny nose the majority of the time. The doc called it chronic sinusitis. I think just sitting down and fully embracing the emotions and recognizing when those emotions need to be expressed is a lot easier. As I have become more proficient in looking at the emotional body, surprise, the chronic sinusitis is gone. It was really unexpressed TEARITIS.

I would like to talk a little about sabotage. When I reflect back on my life I have had many opportunities to move into the fullness of myself, the true greatness of my being. Just when I get to that point, something seems to happen that derails that process. In self-reflection, I see patterns of self-sabotage and my fears of greatness that set up situations that changed my path. I love the quote from Marianne Williamson and feel it reflects some of the path choices that I have made. Are we truly powerful beyond measure? I think so, and for me I think cancer has come into my life to help me understand that truth.

Our Greatest Fear

It is our light not our darkness that most frightens us.
Our deepest fear is not that we are inadequate.
Our deepest fear is that we are powerful beyond measure.
It is our light not our darkness that most frightens us.
We ask ourselves, who am I to be brilliant, gorgeous, talented and fabulous?
Actually, who are you not to be?
You are a child of God.
Your playing small does not serve the world.
There's nothing enlightened about shrinking
so that other people won't feel insecure around you.
We were born to make manifest the glory of God that is within us.
It's not just in some of us; it's in everyone.
And as we let our own light shine,
we unconsciously give other people
permission to do the same.
As we are liberated from our own fear,
Our presence automatically liberates others.

Marianne Williamson
Quote given by Nelson Mandela in a famous speech

Chapter 11

Create Your Day

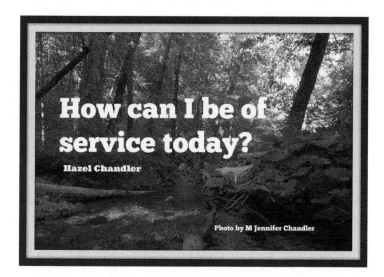

How can I be of service today?

Hazel Chandler

Photo by M Jennifer Chandler

O ne of the most important tools that I have used during this process is to become very clear about creating my day.

Gary Zukav, one of my favorite authors talks about the new scientific method. I really like what he says and think it is really important in creating our day and our life.

1. Be aware of your intentions.
2. Consider what each of your intentions will create.
3. Choose the intentions that will create the consequences you desire. (Responsible choice)
4. Observe how your experiences change.

5. If your experience does not change, find the parts of your personality that hold different intentions and change them.
6. Do the experiments again.

Each day, each moment we have the opportunity to choose again. We have the opportunity to refine our previous creations, be grateful for the lessons that they have provided and become clearer and clearer about our intentions.

I find that waking up in the morning and setting my intentions for the day makes a tremendous difference in the day. Sometimes those intentions are as simple as the statement "God make an instrument of your peace" or "How can I live life to the fullest today" that take only a minute or two before crawling out of bed.

Other days I seem to be led to a more complex process in really looking at my soul's desires and deepest intention. Either way, I believe that getting clear with myself is extremely important in fully showing up for life.

I also believe that at the end of the day a period of reflection is really important to further refine our creation. Taking a look at the flow of life through self-reflection allows us to refine our thoughts and intentions for the next day.

Much has been written about a gratitude journal. I think this is one of the most powerful experiences that one can do to really reflect on life. Sometimes I am really good at writing in a journal and other times not so. I think a simple prayer such as "Thank You" can be as powerful. Learning to live in a place of thankfulness and gratitude for me was a huge piece of moving Beyond the Big C. Gratitude is not a once-a-day event. Bringing gratitude and thankfulness into every moment spurs powerful growth.

Opening and closing each day with intention sets up the energy to allow new life-affirming experiences to manifest in your life. Join with me in the morning and evening energies of creating our day. If the energy of the day seems out of whack, take a few moments to go to the inner space and revise the intention for the day. I have found that closing my door at work, finding a bathroom or going for a little walk provides the space to recreate our intentions. I have found that the simplest intentions work best for me. Something like "How can I serve today?" or "God make me an instrument of your peace" are extremely powerful for getting me back on track.

Chapter 12

Honor Your Body Temple

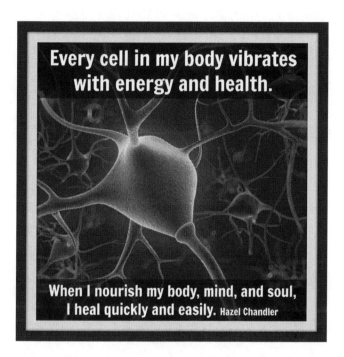

Every cell in my body vibrates with energy and health.

When I nourish my body, mind, and soul, I heal quickly and easily. Hazel Chandler

O
ur bodies are the greatest gift that's given to us. They carry us through life. Unfortunately, most of us in our busy lives give little thought to what our bodies really need to stay healthy and vibrant. We often are unconscious when we stuff food into our body that has no life left in it. We expect the body to keep up with an impossible pace of work and home responsibilities, often with little sleep.

Honoring my body temple is a moment-by-moment process that I feel has been the key to moving beyond the Big C. Taking time to go inside and listen to what my body is telling me is the greatest way that I can honor my body temple. I find the more I take time to listen, the more I am led to people, ideas and treatments that have been instrumental to healing.

Taking the time to eat life-enhancing food, build my immune system and choose to give life to the body temple is critical to living my best life. Each moment we have a new opportunity to choose life, and honoring the role that the body plays is essential in vibrant health. Take time today to listen to what the body wants. Your life depends on it.

Chapter 13

Be Impeccable With Your Words

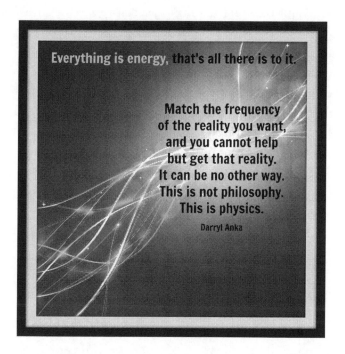

Everything is energy, that's all there is to it.

Match the frequency of the reality you want, and you cannot help but get that reality. It can be no other way. This is not philosophy. This is physics.

Darryl Anka

Our bodies are one of the most mysterious and fascinating subjects of scientific exploration. Contrary to beliefs held through many centuries, science now knows that our bodies are just energy. In fact we are not a solid body but almost 90% empty space. Science also has realized that the act of observing energy can change that energy. If in fact all life is energy, then our words are energy as well. We are in fact powerful beyond our imaginations, and our words and thoughts are creating our own reality

The Bible and most sacred texts talk about the power of the spoken word. "In the beginning was the word and the word was with

God, and the word is God." This quote from the Gospel of John in the Bible is just one of the many references in the sacred texts regarding the power of the word. Another example is in Mark 11-22. "Have faith in God. Truly, I say to you, whoever says to this mountain, 'Be taken up and thrown into the sea,' and does not doubt in his heart, but believes that what he says will come to pass, it will be done for him. Therefore I tell you, whatever you ask in prayer, believe that you have received it, and it will be yours."

Words, both written and spoken, hold a creative power that I am only now beginning to understand. As I journeyed through cancer I was being guided to follow Don Miguel Ruiz's advice in the book the "The Four Agreements" to be impeccable with my words. This included a new level of awareness. As I stated before, one of the big turning points for me was to learn to fully show up in life. Through that process I understood the upmost importance of staying in integrity and through love speaking my truth.

As I really explored the power of words, I came to understand the depth of the impact words have in shaping my life and my beliefs. I heard it said that the word cancer probably killed more people than the disease itself. When we hear the word cancer we automatically associate it with death and dying. The word itself can bring an incredible level of fear that sucks the power from us and sets up opportunities to give our power away to the medical community, family and friends. Each of us has an opportunity to fall under the power of the fear that the word cancer portrays or to rise above and find words that carry a vibration of healing.

I think back to the first surgeon that I saw. When I refused to follow her prescription of immediate surgery, chemo and radiation, she told me that if I did not follow her protocol that I would not live more than six months. What if I had bought her words? Would I be writing these words today? I think not. I am well beyond six months and vibrantly healthy. In fact I am nearing four years.

I think back to my father's journey with cancer. A few days before he died he asked his doctor how long he would live. His doctor's response was probably about a year, but that his health would not get better along the way. I wonder what would have happened if his doctors would have taken another approach. What if they leveled with him that medical science had done all that they could to help him heal, but that there was a power within that had amazing healing power that is beyond explanation. What if they gave him tools to tap into this inner power? Would the outcomes be different? I think they might have been. My dad had a tremendous level of faith, but he had put his faith into his doctors and medication instead of digging deep within his soul to find healing.

From the first moment I learned about my mother's breast cancer I was bombarded by family, friends, media and the medical community with the thought and words that I needed to be especially diligent as breast cancer runs in families. My mother and others were constantly reminding me to get mammograms, as I was at high risk. I wonder how those words influenced cancer setting into my breast. Could the words and thoughts have actually created the cancer? In retrospect I think so. After much exploration into my inner cosmos, I think the unconscious fear of cancer created the experience that we call cancer. Interestingly, the cancer occurred at exactly the same age that my mother was diagnosed.

As I journey through healing, I consciously spend a lot of time observing my words and thoughts. With this heightened sense of observation, I have become acutely aware of my words and the world around me. I am reminded of an analogy that Joel Olsten talks about that we need to protect ourselves from the power of the words of others. He talks about imagining that we have sprayed our body with PAM each morning so the words and thoughts of other do not stick. While I would never use PAM in cooking, maybe it is a good way to visualize others' words and thoughts just bouncing off. PAM in itself is very toxic. Bouncing these toxins right back at the giver seems to be a fair exchange.

Just as we need to be very aware of the impact of the words of others, we need to dig deep within to discover the impacts of others words have hidden in our soul and impact every aspect of our lives.

I think back to third grade. I suddenly had to wear very thick glasses. A number of my friends told me that the glasses were ugly. I think that I internalized that to be that I was ugly. I have struggled with the buried beliefs for most of my life. Words of others, especially to children, can be magic or poison. Don Miguel Ruiz tells us that the words that children hear can be magic to lift the child up or black magic that cast a spell on the child's life. All of us have had spells cast by black magic words on our life, even by well-meaning family, friends and teachers. A parent does not realize the magnitude of the impact words have on a child when in anger they tell a child they are bad or they are ugly. These words get lodged in the depths of the brain and are like a spell that hovers over not only during childhood, but haunts the child into adulthood. Getting to the bottom of these hurts and breaking the spells that were cast by these words is not an easy task, but for me this is extremely important in my healing process.

Finally, I realized how important my words are in creating health. I realized that every word that I speak, write or even think sets up a vibration within the body that can enhance health and create the life I desire to live. Most of us have no idea that we are creating our own reality, as the timeline between the words, thoughts and the actual manifestation of the experience are often delayed by many years.

As I became more aware of my words and thoughts, I experienced many opportunities to realize the power of my thoughts. One example was a few years ago when I traded cars with my daughter so she could take a trip. She was driving my old car with over 230,000 miles on it, and needless to say it was on its last legs. One evening when I pulled it into my parking lot, I had the thought pop into my mind that it would be stolen. I dismissed this as ridiculous – Who would want this piece of ____! The next morning to my horror the car was missing. Who would want a falling apart Integra with 230,000 miles on it? Kind of funny that a lesson about my thoughts creating reality came from a vehicle, and an Integra at that. Was I being ask to have more integrity in my thoughts? Maybe so.

As we move beyond disease, I believe we are required to carefully monitor our words to create a vibrantly healthy future. Rather than talking about our pain, we need to focus on the life we really want to live. Expect God (or whatever you call the creative force that supports life) to do something big in your life. Focus on your passions, your dreams and imagine a vibrantly healthy future with many reasons to live. If you are a parent, imagine your child getting married, or that you are holding a new grandchild. Whatever are your wildest dreams, expect them to become your reality. Take the first step to create the life you have only dreamed of, and I believe you send a message that you need more time on this planet. Living an empowered life is key to health in my book. Use words frequently that affirm this new reality. If someone asks you how you are, respond with fantastic or that you are vibrantly healthy. Be extremely careful about talking about the illness or pain of the journey you are on. While it is important to face your fearful thoughts, you do not need to reinforce those thoughts through the words that you use with the ones that are around you.

See yourself beyond the big C and living the life you want to live. Place words such as "I am blessed," I am vibrant," and "I am healthy" around you as reminders. Use your words to create that life that you always wanted. Life is not over; cancer can be a new doorway.

I love the affirmation from Louise Hayes to use when facing cancer.

Photo by M Jennifer Chandler

Lovingly forgive and release all of the past.

I choose to fill my world with joy. I love and approve of myself. Louise Hayes

Freely use words of love for yourself and your body. When I was working with people with AIDS, I met a wonderful man named Jerry Florence. He had an incredible band called Alliance that had written a number of wonderful uplifting songs that embraced the power of words in our healing process. We made one of his songs a part of every activity that we did at Shanti. The words were not only a powerful healing tool, but using this song in a group established a strong sense of community. I wore out his tapes many years ago, but the words of his songs have stuck with me through the ages. Jerry was one of the incredible men that left this life because of AIDS, but the revenues from his work are still doing healing work today. Spend some time with these words. Sing them to yourself and those around you. I will guarantee that you will change your perspective about yourself and your world.

I Love Myself the Way I am

I love myself the way I am,
there's nothing I need to change
I'll always be the perfect me
there's nothing to rearrange
I'm beautiful and capable
of being the best me I can
And I love myself just the way I am

I love you the way you are
there's nothing you need to do
When I feel the love inside myself
it's easy to love you
Behind your fears, your rage and tears
I see your shining star
And I love you just the way you are

I love the world the way it is,
'cause I can clearly see
That all the things I judge are done
by people just like me
So 'til the birth of peace on earth
that only love can bring
I'll help it grow by loving everything

I love myself the way I am
and still I want to grow.
But change outside can only come
when deep inside I know
I'm beautiful and capable,
of being the best me I can,

And I love myself just the way I am
I love myself just the way I am

Remember that every word that you speak has the power to create your reality. Speak with integrity, and say what you mean. Never use words to speak against yourself or others. Remember the power of your word to create a life filled with truth and love. Be impeccable with your word and watch the power those words carry in creating a healthy happy life.

Chapter 14

Raise the Vibration of Your Body

Faith is taking the first step even when you don't see the whole staircase.

Martin Luther King, Jr.

In this quotation Martin Luther King, Jr. tells us that faith is taking the first step even though we do not have the full picture. For me, I feel that there is a connection between raising the vibration of my body and healing, even though the scientific community has not completely accepted the connection. I believe as we more fully understand the human genome we will more fully comprehend the impacts that our body's frequency has on our health. For me, keeping my body's vibration high was key in my healing process.

Nikola Tesla (1856-1945) is one of the most recognized pioneers of electrical technology. He said that if you could eliminate certain outside frequencies that interfere in our bodies, we would have greater resistance to disease. I think great strides have been made to make the connection to Nikola Tesla theory. The current research at a DNA level is focusing on looking at possible switches that turn on and off the cancer fighting genes in the body. While much work still needs to be done for real breakthrough in research, I think that as people living with cancer it is critical to keep our bodies functioning at the highest vibrational level possible.

Vibrational medicine research is telling us that a healthy body operates between 62 and 72 MHz. When we maintain this optimal frequency, especially of the vibration of the immune system, our bodies are vibrantly healthy. Every day we are bombarded with things that lower our body's frequency such as stress, emotional challenges, low energy foods, medications, electrical magnetic fields as well as the toxic metals, radiation and other toxins that build up in the body. The cumulative impacts of aging can also impact our body's ability to maintain the optimal vibrational level.

Research has shown that when the vibrational level of the body falls below these optimal levels, disease can set in. When the body is operating around 58 MHz, colds, flu and other viral or bacterial issues can set in. Every one of us has experienced a cold during a time when we were highly stressed, overworked and over-tired. In fact this is usually when I experience a cold. Cancer reflects an even lower energy within the body and is thought to be around 42 MHz

The standard American diet (SAD) tends to focus on carbohydrates, fats and protein that are highly processed and void of any vibrational frequency. The foods that we eat can either help or hinder our health. Foods can assist with moving the energy within our body efficiently, provided that we eat the right kinds of food. When we eat wholesome, natural, preferably organic, nutrient-rich, high vibrational food we can maintain or even restore our body's vibration and health. The vibrational frequency of foods resonates with our tissues, cells and organs in a naturally harmonic manner. The resonance between the foods and the various body functions can stimulate and restore our bio-electric fields that promote health.

Foods in their natural state have a vibrational frequency or vital energy that can be measured in hertz. One hertz is one cycle per second of energy flow that is constant between two points.

Canned and processed foods have no energy left in them. This is thought to also be true of genetically modified foods (GMO), which may explain why many of us can eat organic versions of foods, but if we come into contact with the GMO version we have reactions within the body. Fresh food and herbs have a vibrational energy of between 20-27 MHz, while dried foods and herbs vibrate between 15-22 MHz. Fresh vegetables, nuts, legumes, herbs and fruits that are organically grown and eaten when freshly picked have even higher vibrational levels. Fermented vegetable such of Kombucha, Kefir and sauerkraut carry a high frequency as do sea vegetable, wheatgrass, spirulina and blue green algae. When we overcook foods we also lower the vibrational level.

We have many opportunities to raise our body's vibrational level and maintain a level conducive to good health. The first is to eat only foods that nature provides for us in the purest and freshest form possible. Organic fruits, vegetables, herbs and meat provide vibrational support that our bodies need to maintain and restore health. The more we eat fruits and vegetables raw the more energy that we get from our food.

I cannot talk about raising the body's vibrational level without mentioning the critical need for adequate water. Although we get water from our food and drinks, the body needs an abundance of clean water to maintain the vibrational level. I highly recommend that you drink only filtered water, which removes some of the toxins from the water supply. While I spent several years developing a unique form of highly alkaline (micro-water) bottled water, I now question most of the waters on the market. Many are just tap water from some of the most polluted water supplies. We know that the plastic bottles leach BPA and other chemical into the water, especially in hot climates and warm weather. Our bodies need the water to carry the vibration throughout our body and allow energy circuits to fire, keeping the body furnace working at an optional level. To do this most effectively I have found that a good filtered water such as reverse osmosis is probably the best choice. If you can afford to buy a micro-water machine, I encourage you to look into it. Micro-water is known to be absorbed by the cell more effectively than regular waters and has a high alkalinity as well that helps balance the body's PH level.

When we are faced with cancer, we must look deeper into the toolbox for ways to raise the body's vibrational level. Essential oils are an important tool in the toolbox to stabilize and raise the body vibrational level.

Essential Oils have been used throughout history in healing. The bible has many references to the healing power of essential oils. The kings brought gold, frankincense and myrrh to the Christ child. It is believed that the secret to Jesus' healing of the sick had to do with essential oils. Throughout the Bible and other sacred texts, oils were highly regarded and frequently used in the healing process.

We find through Greek, Egyptian and other history that oils were highly treasured. In recent times we have found essential oils buried in the Egyptian tombs. Interestingly enough, oils like frankincense that are thousands of years old are still good and have not lost their vibrational level. Therapeutic grade oils hold frequencies that start around 52 MHz for Basil and can be as high as 320 MHz for Rose oil. Frankincense is one of the highest vibrational oils, and has been shown to be helpful in healing many low-vibrational related conditions. There are a number of articles about frankincense in relation to breast cancer. While my tumors were gone before I found these articles, I think it might be useful to mix frankincense with an organic carrier oil such as almond or even coconut oil and rub it on the breast area. I can use straight frankincense on my body, but for most people it is too strong and burns the skin. I am thinking that cutting the essential oil with an organic carrier is the best method to use this therapy.

It is thought that essential oils do not resonate with the toxins in our bodies or with the negative emotions. The incompatibility helps the body eliminate the toxins through our daily elimination process. It is even thought that they can be helpful in dislodging forgotten traumas by bringing them into our conscious awareness so we can deal with them. I am thinking that this was the case with me. It seemed like the more essential oils that I used the deeper that I dug into the waste pit of forgotten traumas. I remember a couple of times that I said "no more oils." I needed a break from intense emotions, but I would always come back to using oils as they helped me maintain my body energy.

I am not sure if I would have made it to this point without frequent baths that were infused with a variety of essential oils. Or even the diffusers that fill my home with beautiful non-toxic essential oils. My daughter keeps me supplied with oils mixed with water in the form of wellness sprays. Essential oils, mixed with an organic carrier oil release muscle tension and pain. For me these are essential in keeping my body's vibrational level high. When I feel tired, I reach for the oils. When I feel out of sorts I do the same. I use oils in my homemade body care products such as toothpaste, moisturizer, bath salts, etc.

There are a number of other extremely helpful practices that help to raise and maintain the body vibrational level. Meditation, yoga, tai chi, Reiki, breath-work and other techniques all work with the body's vibrational level. For me, getting into nature is also very important in raising my vibrational level. When I exercise out in nature, I become very connected to the natural environment that feeds my soul and raises my vibration. Just climbing my mountain allows energy to flow freely through my body. Thunderbird Mountain is a steep climb, but I come home energized and rejuvenated. Every time of day and season I see the beauty of the desert oasis in the middle of metropolitan Phoenix in a new way. I feel extra power at sunset when the horizon is painted with incredible brush strokes of the sunset in vibrant oranges, reds, yellow and even purple.

Using cell phones, computers and other electronics take a toll on the vibration of our body. I have to take frequent breaks from writing this book, as the use of the computer zaps my energy. We must balance out our time on these electronic devices with active steps to raise our vibrational level.

Look every day for ways to raise the body's vibrational level. Make good choices of foods, and supplements with herbs and essential oils that keep this level high. Take time for meditation (prayer) and exercise. Take breaks from the electronic devices. Your body will thank you.

Chapter 15

Relax into the Flow of the Universe

Always end the day
with POSITIVE THOUGHTS.
No matter how hard things were,
tomorrow is a FRESH opportunity
to make it better. Hazel Chandler

I believe that when we want something the whole universe conspires to help us get it. Unfortunately the universe conspires to give us what we want in response to all of our thoughts. That is true of negative thoughts as well as positive thoughts. In every moment our thoughts are creating the reality we are living in. As we begin to really become aware of our thoughts and refine our wants and desires, we become powerful creators of the life we truly want to live. The universe lines up around us to carry this forward.

I found this to be true in my healing process through cancer. When I recognized this as a powerful lesson on my spiritual journey, I began to notice signs from everywhere that I was on the right path. That was true even on the days that I was feeling my greatest pain.

I was guided to the people and places that could support my journey in the highest way. I would turn on TV or my XM radio and someone would be talking about exactly what I had been facing in my life. I am a huge fan of XM radio, and my favorite channel is Oprah's OM channel, with PBS a close second. Since Oprah's channel is no longer on XM, I have gravitated to Joel Osteen. I invariably found these XM radio stations to be discussing the exact life lesson that I was working on in the moment. Working out of town and traveling across town for my treatments allowed many hours to infuse these wonderful lessons within my being. Messages also come through music, magazine articles, TV shows. Paying attention to what is going on around us and staying open to hear those messages coming from spirit in the form of talk show teachers, entertainers, journalists, etc., is in my opinion how to get direct messages from GOD.

For many years I had grand visions of what my purpose on earth was, but I constantly struggled to make it happen. The universe was frequently reminding me that I was trying to swim upstream and trying to make things happen. In fact our life's work is probably a series of dreams that each build on each other. What I realized is that even though we must move our feet to put things in place, to open our dreams we also need a balance of surrendering the outcome to a force greater than our own. In fact at times we need to relax and ride the flow of the universe.

The experiences that are created may not always look like we expect them, but maybe they are really necessary lessons to take us where we want to go. When I started my journey at Nature Works Best, I somehow had an expectation that healing would happen quickly. With each passing month and MRIs I had to reevaluate my commitment to Vibrant Health and continue to relax into the flow of the universe.

When we are clear with what we want the universe moves us towards it, but not always on the time schedule that we have in mind. I firmly believe that my internal fears and resistance to look at the fears slowed my own healing process.

Sometime seeds are planted that do not grow for many years. In fact many of the insights of this book have grown from seeds planted over twenty years ago. I edited it and brought some of the insights up to date, but most of the messages are still important today.

I believe that our thoughts and wishes create many detours, but the universe is always nudging us to keep moving forward. Diagnosis with cancer is one of those nudges, challenging me to reconnect with the sacred contract of my life.

Paulo Coelo in the "The Alchemist" talks about this sacred contract as our personal legend. I believe everyone has a personal legend. We are here to discover our own personal legend and live in accordance with the legend. I believe cancer came into my life to guide me to my personal legend, and to that I am truly grateful.

I firmly believe that the reason all of us are here is to honor the miracle of love. This I believe is built into each of our personal legends. Relaxing in the flow requires us to realize that every one of us here has a reason to be here, and we can dance together in the flow of life. Those parts of our self and those around us who seem to have lost their ways are keys to where we are betraying our personal legend. Through loving we can open the flow in our life, as well as give permission to others to do the same.

A sign we are in the flow is when everything that we do is with passion and enthusiasm. When I have a clear heart the universe course-corrects for me. Remember that cancer is our unfulfilled dream eating away at us. It is having the dream, but not having the courage to be able to step out and fulfill that dream. Our fear keeps us from our dream. As I stated before, fear is the cells gone wild in our body. Having the courage to change our perspective and take back control of our life allows life to open up to us.

Don't give into your fears, for if you do, you will not be able to communicate with your heart. The universe is teaching us the right signs – Listen to the body, the rhythms of the universe. Start really listening to life. I believe this is the root to healing and turning on the Vibrant Health switch.

Before a dream is realized the soul is tested along the way. Giving the gifts of life-threatening illness is a test of the strength to move the dream forward. As we listen to our heart and the authentic self within and stand in our authentic power, we unleash the support of the universal flow of life.

Chapter 16

Live Life

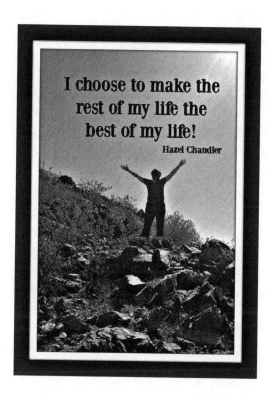

A s I talked about in Chapter 1, the dreaded phone call from my nurse practitioners with the diagnosis of Breast Cancer was a huge wake-up call. She said that I needed to see an oncologist and a surgeon immediately. I knew intuitively that this was indeed serious, and I should not delay getting an appointment. I also requested a copy of the pathology report, so I would have a better understanding of what I was dealing with.

In taking a closer look at the pathology reports, I found that the cancer was invasive lobular carcinoma, pleomorphic type, and probably stage 3. The five separate tumors covering most of the breast, including the nipple, were Estrogen and Progesterone and HER-2 positive. I took a deep breath and had a moment of panic. An internet search about this type of cancer revealed that this is a fast growing cancer, with mixed results with any treatment. I knew this was a **BIGGGGGG LESSON.** My stomached tied in knots and mild panic set in.

Within a couple of days I had an appointment with a recommended surgeon. The appointment with the surgeon did nothing to ease that panic, as she wanted to do a radical mastectomy, chemo and radiation immediately. She said that was the only choice if I wanted to live. I took a deep breath and said thank you very much for your opinion; I believe I need a second opinion. She told me that if I delayed treatment I would probably not make it. Probably not more than six months.

Again, I thanked her very much for her opinion, but knew this was not a road that I wished to travel. To be fair to her, she had recently come through her own journey with breast cancer, and I feel that she was projecting some of her fears on me.

Deep inside of me, my body was telling me there had to be another way. A way to love my body back to health, not declare war on my body. At the core of my being I was devoted to peaceful existence, and declaring war on my body did not seem to be congruent with my belief system.

When I went to the internet, the first thing that came up in my search for alternatives was Nature Works Best. I immediately made the decision to go the route of building my immune system, using food, vitamins and herbal formulas to love my body back to health. What I found on this internet site was in total alignment with what my inner guidance was telling would be the path to healing.

Lori at Nature Works Best, the first voice, was so loving and helpful with scheduling the first appointment and getting the paperwork completed I knew immediately that I had found the right place.

At my first appointment, my doctor got a complete health history, reviewed the pathology reports and other medical records that I had provided. They also ordered numerous blood work screens, some were typical of allopathic medicine, but also some specialized tests to measure inflammation, thyroid function, hormone level and specialized breast cancer tests.

After much discussion and the opportunity to get to know my doctor, in a way that I had never experienced with any other doctors, we together developed a plan for healing. The difference between this experience and past experiences was that all of the staff at this clinic, including the doctors, really cared about my well-being and were willing to become partners with me in my healing journey.

I was immediately scheduled to begin IV therapy three times a week. Walking in the IV room, I was greeted by amazing people that were walking the same journey as I was. Sometimes I think that the bonds that form within the IV room are as important to the healing results this amazing clinic is obtaining as the treatments themselves.

The intravenous nutrients are tailored specifically to each patient's condition and chosen for their targeted, time tested, and research-documented anti-cancer, **cancer fighting** effect. The nutrients that the doctors use are different for each patient, but some of nutrients used may include a combination of Vitamin-C, Sodium Bicarbonate, Glutathione, DMSO, with vitamins, minerals and herbal cancer inhibiting substances.

The exact formula for the IV differs with each type/stage of cancer and each patient. My IV was specific to my type of cancer, to my overall medical needs, and the formulation changed with each appointment to respond to my body's needs and any symptoms that I was experiencing. I knew that this was an **alternative treatment to chemo and radiation that was right for me.**

This treatment made my body strong, allowing me full control of my life force energy—contrary to what I had experienced with both my parents and other friends that have had their own journey with cancer using the medical standard of treatment. My individualized treatment protocol included an array of vitamins, minerals, herbs and other supplements designed to stop the growth of the cancer cells. Most of all, I was given a specific eating plan that I call my Live-It that was recommended that I adopt for life.

It would be great to report that after three months the cancer was totally gone. My first MRI after starting treatment revealed little change to the tumors. It would be easy to get discouraged, but with HER-2 positive cancer I saw that as a great sign. This went on for a year. Every three months I would have a MRI and each time was confronted by many fears. I questioned all of the decisions that I had made, but always came back to knowing that a source greater than myself was at work in my body and that source knew what was best for me.

My doctors helped me work through the emotion, each time giving me the option to have a mastectomy. In every case the decision was mine. I would go inside, get quiet and listen to the inner voice, and it was always not now. As the year anniversary of my diagnosis arrived and the tumors were still there, I made an extremely challenging decision to do surgery. When I got quiet I felt strongly that the time was right.

I had found a new surgeon that had worked with many of my doctor's patients. She told me that I would need a radical mastectomy, and since there were indications that the cancer had been in the lymph nodes that she would probably would have to remove the lymph nodes as well. She felt due to the type of cancer, immediate reconstruction was not recommended. I believe her medical mind was thinking that after months of delay she would have a complicated surgery ahead of her.

Throughout the process of scheduling the surgery, I stayed in my power around all of the decisions. In the past I have had problems with anesthesia and pain medication. I discussed this with the doctor, and she made the choice to schedule the surgery when her favorite anesthesiologist was available and honored my request for the absolute minimum of pain medications. I also requested that my doctor do a sentinel node biopsy before removing lymph nodes.

I took a couple of days off to prepare for the surgery, spending the time in meditation and setting an intent that the surgery would be the last step in the healing process. On the morning of the surgery, I had to arrive several hours early so that my doctor could insert the dye into sentinel node. I spent the entire time in meditation and reading my favorite inspiring authors and calling in healing angels to help out. I also had a talk with the anesthesiologist about my concerns with anesthesia and pain medications, and he assured me that he would use only the absolute minimum necessary.

I awoke within 15 minutes of leaving the operating room, fully alert and able to discuss the great news with my daughter and doctor. She only needed to do a simple mastectomy, removing only one sentinel node for biopsy. She said she had an extremely easy time in getting clear margins as the tumors were encapsulated in what she called a hard shell. The cancer appeared to be totally contained and probably was no longer growing. Further results indicated that all of the cancer was totally contained within the removed tumors.

If I would have known that the cancer was locked into the tumors with a hard shell, I might have decided not to do the surgery, but we make the best decisions with the information that we have. I have since read recent research that indicates that tumors may be protective shields that prevent the cancer stem cells from affecting the body. Since the tumors were not growing I question if the surgery was really necessary, but I know that we make the best decisions we can with the information that we have.

Most of my life I have had body image issues. Maybe this is an opportunity to love my body, with only one boob. I found it interesting that it almost seemed to be easier to love my body after the surgery than it was before. I don't know what shifted, but something seemed to shift.

My healing was nothing short of amazing. I was in my room at the hospital within an hour of coming out of surgery, which was around five in the evening. I was up walking the halls immediately. Within a couple of hours I had normal bowel and urine flow. I refused all medications. Vitals were perfect. I insisted that my IV be removed, and after threatening to remove it myself, my nurse finally did so. I had to protect my precious veins at all costs.

The hospital menu had nothing that I would put into my body, so I sent my daughter for healthy food and ate a full meal. At 8:00 the next morning I went home. That evening I attended my grandson's birthday party. I did not need a single pain medication, and even though I took a few days off of work, I felt really great. The wound healed very quickly. I believe the treatments that I received were instrumental not only in the quick healing, but the wonderful outcome. I have had several MRIs since and no evidence of any cancer.

The team approach that allowed me to retain my power and make the decisions that were right for me was critical in my healing process. I am extremely grateful to everyone that has helped in the healing process, providing support, love and encouragement, but allowing me to walk my own journey.

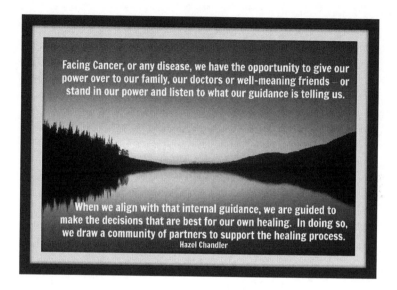

Facing Cancer, or any disease, we have the opportunity to give our power over to our family, our doctors or well-meaning friends — or stand in our power and listen to what our guidance is telling us.

When we align with that internal guidance, we are guided to make the decisions that are best for our own healing. In doing so, we draw a community of partners to support the healing process.
Hazel Chandler

Chapter 17

Live Sugar Free

We can choose to live life or die life. The choice is yours!!

Hazel Chandler

Before meeting with the Nature Works Best I had read extensively about the connection between sugar and cancer. Cancer needs sugar to grow, so when we eat sugar we are feeding the cancer cells. My doctor confirmed what I already knew about the role of sugar in the growth of cancer cells. Although I had been interested in healthy eating for many years, I realized in the past couple of years with the stress of extensive work, travel and restaurant food, I was craving carbs and sugar. Responding to these cravings with carbs and sugar probably contributed significantly to the growth of the cancer cells.

Most of my travel was to an area that you safely could call a healthy food desert. While there are restaurants and grocery stores in the area, finding healthy food is extremely difficult.

When McDonald's and Subway are some of the healthiest choices, you know you have a problem. With the lack of choices and cooking facilities, I often resorted to a fast food lunch, which left me lacking energy to face the afternoon work schedule. Many days my breakfast was a Starbucks coffee and a muffin. The stress of the mid-afternoons saw me running across the street to get a candy bar on a pretty regular basis.

I knew that one of the first steps in loving my body back to health was to make choices that allowed my body to have the fuel necessary to heal, including focusing on life-enhancing foods.

With that first appointment with Nature Works Best, I made it my first priority to live life fully. I agreed to totally eliminate sugar, flour and refined foods and focus on healthy vegetables, low sugar fruits, organic free-range meats and whole grains such quinoa, oats and amaranth. I chose to call the eating plan a **LIV-IT**, not a diet. With every cell of my body I wanted to **live life fully**, not die life.

I made a decision right then to show up fully in my life and enjoy each moment. When I was focused on that moment it was easy to make good decisions. In that moment, I could be grateful for the feeling of life in my body and take an opportunity to affirm life. Making a decision to never eat sugar or refined grains seemed like an impossible hurdle, but it was easy to make life-affirming decisions in the moment and make a good food choices.

When I am faced with a choice of a healthy or unhealthy food, I take a moment to take a deep breath and affirm that I choose life. What I have found is that action of bringing myself into the moment and making a life-affirming choice dissipates the desire for the unhealthy food. That brownie no longer looks good.

Sugar is an addiction just like alcohol and drugs. Just like the successful treatment for drug and alcohol requires the addict to make the decision in each moment not to drink or use, sugar also requires the same commitment. Sugar addiction requires millions of little decisions to honor your body and choose a vibrant life.

Just like the addict has pressure from peers to drink or use again, the people around me sometimes did not totally understand the road to health that I chose to walk. Sometimes friends and family would make comments such as "a little bit won't hurt" or "have just a couple of bites."

With cancer the couple of bites can fuel the cancer growth, not to mention start the craving cycle all over again. What I also found is that eating a couple bites would also leave me feeling heavy the next day and frequently would flare up the cancer pain. For me it was really important to stand strong to live life fully, make good choices – even if the people around me did not fully understand. What I have found over the last couple of years is that those around me are also making better choices for themselves.

In each moment we choose love or fear. When fear comes up – ask what the fear wants to tell us – listen, release and fill with love.
Hazel Chandler

Another big factor in my healing was to make friends with my fears. It was extremely important not to stuff the fears, but to take time when the fear comes up to fully examine that fear and allow that fear to pass on through. For me one of the big opportunities to face my fears was to openly talk about my journey to vibrant health. The first fear that came up was that if I shared what I was going through it might impact my job or other people's opinion of me, especially since I was 67 years old and most people my age are already retired. Openly talking about my journey has allowed me to face many of those fears in myself, but also to allow my friends and family to work through their own fears, especially around the treatment protocol that I chose.

Another fear was "what if it did not work?" I was more afraid of what other people would think if I failed than the potential outcome. Having worked with people with terminal illness, I do not fear death and believe that life continues—just in another form.

I feel that facing fears was also a very important part of my decision to make good food choices. If each decision to eat healthy was made from a place of fear that the cancer would grow, I believe that it could have impacted the results. I believe that the energy that we put out comes back to us. I did not want to make my eating choice to be about fear. Instead I chose to make the choices not from fear but from love for my body; I wanted to give it everything that it needed to live a healthy vibrant life. I was making a choice to **live life** not to die life.

My eating plan was a **LIV-IT**, not a die-it. This was being reaffirmed with every food decision that I was making. This was kind of a vote for life. Staying in the moment and choosing to live life fully made each of the choices more manageable. When I could stay in the moment, my mind was not focused on the future "what if," but savoring the small things such as the beauty of the greens that I was putting into my shake or the pattern of the bubbles as my quinoa was cooking on the stove or lovingly nurturing the herbs that I was growing on my patio.

Today, almost two years later, I am totally cancer free. When I reflect over the last two years, I realize that I am probably more vibrantly alive than I have ever been in my life. This was true throughout the journey. Although I initially slowed down a little on the work hours to give my body the rest that it needed to begin healing, I have continued to work full-time, traveled extensively with my job and maintained every aspect of a vibrant life. I am extremely grateful to have a work situation that allowed me the flexibility to do the regular treatments, which were an extreme-ly important part of the protocol. I maintained the energy and passion for life throughout my treatment, which allowed me to complete my work early in the morning and/or later in the day so that I could fulfill my full-time job commitments.

With the requirement of my position to travel three to four days a week, I have had to be extremely creative in making the choice of foods that enhanced my life. If you have ever tried to find healthy food in Globe, Arizona, you will fully understand the challenge of this endeavor. Traveling with food in Arizona, especially in the summer months, adds to this challenge. One of the things that I came to understand was that I needed to find ways to carry my food with me or to buy foods at the local grocery store that would supplement the foods that I could carry.

One the first steps was to make friends with the produce man-ager in the local grocery store. When I first went to Globe, the produce manager did not seem to even understand what I was requesting when I asked for organic vegetables. The first step was getting him to order organic spinach and salad mix, which were extremely difficult to carry between Phoenix and Globe.

Now I have a small selection of organic produce, including spin-ach, several organic salad mixes, kale, carrots, sometimes berries

and other produce to choose from at the local Safeway. Not anything like what you can get in the valley, but it seems to be getting
better every day. I also supplement with other vegetables that are
on the list of foods that do not have as many pesticides and are
safer to eat in the non-organic form.

Another important piece was to cook healthy dishes such as len-
til soup, beans, chicken curry, and other soups and stews that I
could carry with me.

I choose not to use microwave ovens, so heating these has been a
challenge. I have found that toaster ovens heat foods, although it
just takes a little more time.

I also try to make sure much of my **LIV-IT** is fresh foods eaten in
their natural form. I have learned to love asparagus and brussels
sprouts raw. They make a great addition to a salad or are great for
snacking mid-afternoon. Carrot sticks with hummus is another
great option for snacking. (Watch the ingredients in store hummus as many have canola oil or other oils – use only hummus
made with olive oil.) I carry lemons, apple cider or coconut vinegar with me, which allows me to mix in a little olive oil and
have a healthy dressing for my salads. Keeping nuts on hand for
snacks or to add to the salads also has been very helpful.

I have also found that the good grains such as quinoa, buckwheat
and other ancient grains travel well and are great mixed with
some chopped vegetables. Adding maybe a little vinegar, lemon
juice or even sections of a cutie (tangerine) to spark up the taste
make this a great refreshing and filling lunch. These same grains
can be mixed with berries, nuts and maybe a little cinnamon for
a delicious, nutritious breakfast. A sprinkle of chia or flax seeds
is also a good nutritious addition, adding the very important
omega 3 oils and additional fiber. These ancient grains are rich in
protein and fiber, and they are very low on the glycemic index,
making them very good food choices that are filling and very

healthy. Chicken, meat or fish can be added, but this is a healthy lunch or breakfast without the added protein.

Another important part of the **LIV-IT** is juicing. I choose to use a Vitamix that allows me to turn whole fruits and vegetable into delicious vegetable juices and shakes. I regularly juice when I am home, but it was a little tricky to find ways to include juice into my travel routine. While it is always best to have absolutely fresh juice, juice that is refrigerated or frozen in an airtight glass container is the next best thing.

Prior to any travel, I make huge batches of juice. I use canning jars to bottle the juice. I place a couple in the refrigerator to enjoy on my morning drive to Globe. I leave at 5:30 a.m., so it is a very early morning drive. I freeze several more glass containers of juice. The key to freezing juice in glass containers is to leave the lids off until the juice freezes. The expansion in freezing can break a covered glass container. When I am ready to leave, I put the frozen containers in with my other foods that I am taking with me in my ice chest. The frozen juices help keep the other foods cold. When I arrive I put most of the juice in the refrigerator to thaw slowly. I leave one out to thaw to drink with lunch. Since it can take a day or so for the juice to thaw in the refrigerator, I usually can have fresh juice for at least a couple of days.

Another important step is to find a restaurant that is open to cooking foods in a special way. I found a chef that will prepare chicken fajitas with lots of peppers, tomatoes and onions in a small amount of butter or olive oil. In fact he bought olive oil to honor my request. I learned that it is extremely important to ask for what we need. Healthy choices of additional items that you put on the fajitas makes this a much better choice than most of the Globe area Mexican restaurants. I have asked a lot of questions about the Pico de Gallo and the guacamole. At this restaurant neither of these contains any sugars. As a result, this is a satisfying tasty dish. Maybe this is not a perfect fit to the **LIV-IT**, but much healthier than other choices. I make sure that I affirm this healthy choice, show how grateful I am to the staff for preparing and serving this food to me. I take time to bless the food as I eat it. I firmly believe that this can enhance the body's ability to use the food to enhance life.

Much has been written about the power of loving thoughts and prayer in the healing process. Prayer and loving thoughts has even been shown to affect the molecular structure of water. If you look at the research around water, you can see the amazing impact of these prayers and thoughts on the way water molecules cluster. Loving, grateful thoughts can actually change water. I have seen this firsthand with the wonderful work of Masaru Emoto, who has done extensive work to photograph water clusters. I believe that blessing our foods and sending loving thoughts also help the energy contained within the food to be more useful to the body.

The challenges of healthy eating on the go are many, especially in Globe. Although I have made some inroads with one of the Mexican Restaurants, I haven't even tried to find a healthy alternative at the two Chinese restaurants. They are next on this list. Subway can make a good salad with lots of veggies. Maybe the food is not organic, but a better choice in a pinch than some of the other choices.

Here in the Phoenix area, we have more choices, but we have to be very careful to choose wisely from menu options and ask lots of questions about how a dish is prepared. We need to feel free to ask for our specific dietary needs to be met. If a restaurant will not or cannot meet our needs we do not have to eat there.

I firmly believe that the numbers of people that are interested in healthy eating are transforming our stores and restaurants. Health Food stores are in a massive growth mode, and the healthy sections of our grocery stores are expanding every day. Restaurants are adding healthier options to menus as well as many are opening that are focusing on fresh real locally grown food pre-pared in a natural healthy way.

When considering treatment options, each of us needs to become well informed regarding all of the options, including potential side effects. Each of us needs to find the option that works best for us. My journey may not be right for everyone, but I hope that you will at least find out more about natural alternatives either as a combination with traditional treatment or as a journey towards healing.

One of the things that all of us need to ask about are the benefits and side effects of the treatment options. I would love to share with you the side effects that I have experienced. Let me tell you about the side effects of my **LIV-IT** and natural treatments I have received the last two years.

I have a fantastic body. I lost over 30 unwanted pounds and am currently wearing clothes that I wore in my 30s. I have vibrant energy that allows me to fully show up for life and maintain a busy work/life balance. I can keep up with my 9- and 11-year-old grandsons in walks and hikes. One of my grandsons challenges me to longer and longer walks.

I had been plagued for many years with significant body pain, especially in my knees, which was probably arthritic in nature. When I first started the treatment, I had a few days that it went from bad to worse even making it a little hard to walk, but after a few days the toxins left my body and I have very few if any body pains today.

My skin and nails grow quickly. Many people have commented on how much more vibrant my skin has become.

I recently had an eye doctor's appointment, and my eyesight has improved dramatically, requiring a significant decrease in my prescription lens strength. I have worn very strong glasses since I was in third grade. In fact even with my genetic history of pressure in my eye, my eye doctor has removed me from the risk list for pressure-related issues such as glaucoma which had been identified several years ago. The cataracts' growth has completely reversed in the past few years.

I have an incredible immune system. I have not had a cold, flu or respiratory issue since I started the treatments over two years ago. Previous allergies are greatly reduced, and when I am strict with the eating plan they do not affect me. If allergy symptoms show up at all I evaluate everything that I have eaten. I can usually find the issue and have the opportunity to change that. Often it is hidden wheat or dairy in foods. This is extremely challenging to monitor if you eat in a restaurant.

My digestive system has been an issue for many years. In younger years, I was diagnosed with a spastic colon. Since beginning this **LIV-IT** my entire digestive system works extremely well. Even with large amount of beans and veggies, I seldom experience gas and bloating.

Did I have times that the cancer caused pain and discomfort? **Absolutely**. When those symptoms came up I would ask my body if there was a message in the pain that I was experiencing. I frequently seemed to get a message, and when I listened the pain disappeared. I could go on forever about the side effects or lack thereof.

Remember that your healing and vibrant living is in your hands. Keeping focused on living gives us the courage to face the choices in front of us. No matter what you chose, remember that choosing life-enhancing lifestyle and food choices will make the prognosis better, no matter the choices that you make in your life journey. Learning to face your own mortality allows us to fully live our life.

Remember:

1. Choose Life.
2. Take time to honor yourself and your needs.
3. Choose what you put in your mouth carefully – Treat sugar and refined carbs as if they were a toxin.
4. Consider the treatment options, and choose what is right for you. Do not let anyone take your power away.
5. Love yourself, and allow those around you to love you.
6. Remember that life is a terminal illness. None of us gets out of it alive. Treat each moment as if it might be your last. Do not go to bed with words unsaid or relationships that need to be healed. Focus on living life each day, rather than fear death.
7. Make sure to make time for your "Bucket List."
8. Affirm daily that you are vibrantly healthy (even when you sometimes do not feel that way). Find little ways that affirm your vibrancy – even though it might just be that you can walk to the end of the block.
9. Have fun and enjoy life.

Chapter 18

Courage to Live an Inspired Life

OUR INTENTION
CREATES OUR
REALITY. " Dr. Wayne W. Dyer

Photo by M. Jennifer Chandler

"Although we may not be aware of who or what is moving the checkers, life has a purpose, and each step of our journey has something to teach us. I wasn't aware of all of the future implications that these early experiences were to offer me. Now, from a position of being able to see much more clearly, I know that every single encounter, every challenge, and every situation are all spectacular threads in the tapestry that represents and defines my life, and I am deeply grateful for all of it." Dr. Wayne W. Dyer

It is now almost four years from the my original diagnosis and several months since I have written most of this book. I continue to live vibrantly healthy cancer free life. I have also taken a leap of faith toward fully living the life I had always dreamed of. As the late Wayne Dyer says, I am looking forward to the spectacular threads in the tapestry that defines my life. I am so grateful for every experience I have had during the journey through cancer.

I have always been a huge fan of Wayne Dyer. I first found his work in the early 80s. At that time he was teaching empowerment in the business world. I spent a lot of time in the car listening to tapes of his workshops. Over the years I have followed the works of this great author on his own journey to healing. He as well has had the gift of cancer on this journey of life. Wayne and other authors have given me the courage to take the next step in living an inspired life. In the end, Wayne left this world cancer-free. His contract was completed.

Through the summer and fall of 2014, I had a strong urging that it was time to honor myself fully and move my life into my next step on life's journey. I was being called to write and share my story as well as honor my body's needs for rest, healthy foods, exercise and just time to be. Although I loved my job with First Things First and felt inspired by the work that I was doing in the community, the extensive travel and being away from home three to four nights a week made it difficult to really listen to what my body needed. I knew that I was being called in a new direction, but struggled with making a decision to move on. Some of the internal dialogue was: How would I survive without my paycheck? What if I lost my good medical insurance that helped pay for part of my treatment? What if I got sick and had no sick leave?

Because I was never really sick with cancer I had six weeks or more of sick leave I had not used. Therefore, I took time in the fall of 2014 to really listen to that inner dialogue and ask for clear guidance about how to address the inner conflict. I got very clearly that my work with First Things First was complete and that I should turn in my notice to retire with adequate time to ensure that a smooth transition could be made for a new staff person to carry on the work that had been started. Around my birthday, I asked for clear guidance and was given two dates. I was to turn in my notice on October 22, 2014 and was to fully retire on my seventh year anniversary with First Things First on March 3, 2015.

Initially I thought that the time would give me an opportunity to create something to take its place. I thought I would use some of the sick leave and vacation that I had to create my next step and move gracefully into the new invention of myself. Well I guess that was not in the cards. The retirement time came with a flurry of celebrations, but also a rush of projects that I felt I had to complete. My retirement date came with no clear path to my next step. I knew I was being asked to just trust.

Initially I gravitated toward a non-profit that I had helped to form, but deep down I had a strong feeling that this was not really my highest path. When I put time into this project it felt that I was trying to swim upstream. When I really made a list of my favorite things to do, fundraising somehow made the bottom of the list. The model that we had created would require massive fundraising efforts as our mission was to help people pay for Naturopathic treatments which were very expensive. Our efforts to fundraise felt to me like we were swimming upstream. (Please note that now that this book is done, I have found another way to move this non-profit forward. Some of the proceeds from this book will support the Naturopathic Cancer Society to help people to have a choice in their treatment. Often surrendering to a greater flow is the key to moving things forward.) I believe that my inner spirit was asking me to choose to live a life where I honor the inner yearnings and vision. I was being asked to move forward with my personal inner power to create a life that was self-honoring and honoring to everyone around me. I knew it was time to be honest with the board and allow someone else to carry this project forward. Now was my time to create my life from the depths of my soul, not with someone else's expectation of me.

I was getting clear messages from within that I was to just be. It was time to experience being, not doing. It was time to concentrate on taking care of myself as my first role. For a couple of months I did little but take care of myself. I spent three to four hours a day in meditation, self-reflection and study. Exercise, good nutrition and self-care became my primary responsibility. I felt deep flow of life force within me – maybe feeling truly alive for the first time. Living in the moment and trusting that my needs would be met was my biggest lesson, but for the first time it was becoming easy. This has been a time to become truly aware of my thoughts and my fears.

My journey towards healing was based on loving my body and listening to my needs. For much of the cancer journey, I could only use peaceful words, avoiding such words as fighting and even warrior. As I moved through my self-reflection I began to realize being a warrior has many meanings. We have the choice to fight and become a warrior out of fear or out of love. The energy is very different. What I realized through my journey through cancer was that I had become a warrior for love. Through this process I had become confident and able to stand up for who I am and who I am destined to be. I aligned with divine energy within that gave me the courage to move forward, choosing strength over weakness. It allowed me to realize the power each of us has within us.

In fact as we move through our fears, emotional challenges and take a stand for life we become warriors, not victims, and fighters instead of followers. We are being asked every day to light our heart on fire, tap into the divine truth within to heal ourselves and everyone around us. We are learning to tap into an innate wisdom that has always been hidden within us. The same inner strength is what we call upon when we need to protect our child. I believe that inner strength is the key to healing. What if learning every day to tap into the inner strength, speak our truth and love ourselves and everyone around us is the key to healing? For me I think it was. Ask yourself how you can tap into that divine within and create the life that you have only dreamed of. As you move forward from this place of power, love and strength suddenly you truly (maybe for the first time) live life.

Chapter 19

Apollo Moon Shot for Cancer
Will it Work?

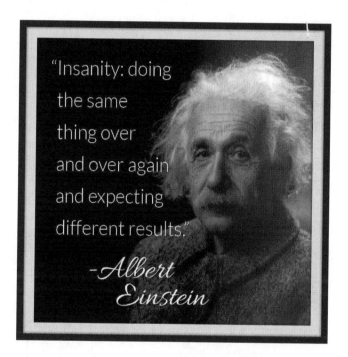

"Insanity: doing the same thing over and over again and expecting different results."

-Albert Einstein

When President Obama, in his final State of the Union address, launched an Apollo like Moonshot-effort to cure cancer, many thousands of cancer patients, survivors and their love ones cheered. The efforts of the Apollo missions to put a man on the moon in the 60s conjure up awe-inspiring images and a symbol of power and ingenuity of the American people. It also shows what we can accomplish when we bring the brightest in our culture together towards a common goal. Putting Vice President Joe Biden (who lost his son to brain cancer) in charge brings a high commitment and passion to this effort, but the question remains: Is this going to be successful? I highly respect President Obama's and Vice President Biden's commitment to this effort, but I have some real concerns about the potential outcomes.

Albert Einstein is credited with the above quote regarding the definition of insanity. What we have been doing with regards to cancer for the last 50 years has concentrated on declaring war on cancer, using highly toxic treatments that we now know do not work. We now know that chemotherapy kills cancer patients faster than no treatment at all, but the medical/pharmaceutical industry has been slow to change as cancer treatment is a huge economic driver. In other words, the drive for profits has kept us locked into a system that does not work. Will this effort be more of the same insanity with the expectation of different result? I hope this will not be the case, but as a cancer survivor, I am extremely concerned that the powerful medical and pharmaceutical industry will take control of this effort, and we will have more of the same. Or even worse, in the name of protecting people, rules will be developed that tie the hands of Naturopaths and other natural practitioners that limit our choices in the treatment we use in our healing process.

In Arizona the medical board tried to prevent Naturopaths from using one of the substances that was extremely important to my healing process and my Naturopath's success with hundreds of patients in spite of absolutely no evidence of any side effects— except helping people to heal.

The new Compounding Pharmacy regulations are making it more and more difficult and expensive for my doctor and others to treat using the protocols that helped in my healing. These new regulations limit the physician's ability to compound in their office. They also require preservatives to be added to substances that are compounded by a pharmacy even though all of the acceptable preservatives are known potential carcinogens. To me this falls under the definition of insanity.

What do we know about Cancer? We know that in 1900 only one in 100 got cancer. By 1950 that number was about 1 in 50. Today one in three women and one in two men are expected to have cancer in their lifetime.

Recent DNA research indicates that cancer may not be a disease in the traditional sense at all. We are discovering that cancer is not one disease, but 100s of separate unique manifestations that have been lumped into one disease category with a one-size-fits-all treatment protocol. We have now identified over 80 unique forms of breast cancer alone. Does it seem a little insane to believe that one standard treatment protocol will be effective for 100s of forms of cancer? I think so.

A 2013 report from National Cancer Institute in the American Medical Journal (JAMA) states that over-diagnosis and misdi-agnosis are thought to be two major causes of the growing can-cer epidemic. For instance, many women are diagnosed with a breast cancer that is not breast cancer at all, but a benign con-dition called *ductal carcinoma in situ* (DCIS). Millions of men are diagnosed with certain forms of prostate issues that are a precursor to cancer, but are treated with highly toxic treatment protocols as if they were cancer. The initial treatments for these misdiagnosed benign conditions with toxic cancer-causing che-motherapy is known to cause more aggressive cancers to occur.

A recent study was published in the journal *"Transaction of the New York Academy of Science"* by Dr. Hardin Jones, a former professor of physics and physiology at University of California, Berkley. He has been studying lifespans of cancer patients for more than 25 years. He has concluded that chemotherapy does not work. He watched multitudes of cancer patients die horrific deaths from chemo. He said that people who refused treatment lived for an average of 12 ½ years, while those who accepted treatment lived only an average of three years. This is true for breast cancer where he found that women who were left untreated lived four times longer than those who agreed to be poisoned with chemicals.

In the words of the National Cancer Institute, the practice of oncology in the United States "is in need of a host of reforms and initiatives to mitigate the problem of over-diagnosis and over-treatment of cancer."

What if cancer was really the body's attempt to survive living in a highly toxic world? What if it was a result of a body deficient in nutrition, overburdened by carcinogens, radiation, toxic food, household items, body care products and even the air we breathe, the water we drink and earth itself that we walk on? What if cancer was just a barometer to help us respond to this harmful onslaught?

I firmly believe that cancer is the body's attempt to survive this toxic physical and emotional burden that our bodies are carrying. Studies of our bodies show that we are toxic waste sites that store the toxins that we are exposed to every single day. We have over 80,000 chemicals that are in our everyday life, but less than 200 have fully studied to determine their safety. Many of those that have been studied are known carcinogens, but they are still on the market and in everyday use. Even those that have been studied are looked at as individual chemicals, not an ingredient in a toxic soup mixed together. When we combine the impacts that the environmental factors have on our bodies, with the stresses and pressures of everyday life we have a recipe that may in fact create our body's cry to survive, which we have labeled cancer. What if cancer was a wake-up call to listen to our bodies and clean-up the toxic waste site that we have created internally?

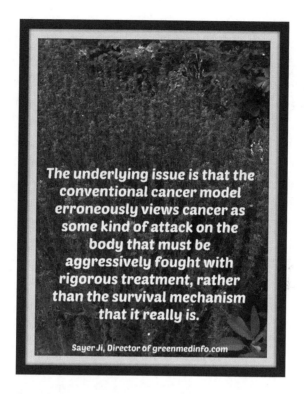

The underlying issue is that the conventional cancer model erroneously views cancer as some kind of attack on the body that must be aggressively fought with rigorous treatment, rather than the survival mechanism that it really is.

Sayer Ji, Director of greenmedinfo.com

What if this "Cancer Moonshot" created a new paradigm for looking at the task in front of us that focused in a much more holistic way at the issues? What if the leaders mobilized the masses to change the ways we interact with the world and each other?

What if we brought all of the medical community, pharmaceutical companies, supplement companies, and integrative medical providers together with people living with cancer and agree on one thing: That is that we are going to put everything on the table. We are going to tell the truth even if it impacts our business. We are going to commit to work side-by-side with physicians, naturopaths, chiropractors, acupuncturists, nutritionists, environmental practitioners and people living with all kinds of cancers committed to one thing—finding a way to end cancer. As people living with cancer we must commit to take personal responsibility for our health. Our team of providers will work together to empower us to find our own vibrant health. The focus is on empowering each us to move Beyond the Big C or—even better—to prevent it in the first place. Then I believe we will have a successful moonshot for cancer. When money, profits, and politics can be removed from the equation, we will be able to really look with new eyes and find what is right in front of us. We have approached cancer from a place of fear and have declared war on it, but in fact I believe the answers are rooted in love and peace. I believe the key is to build the body immune system, not kill it. When we act in love we find ways to come together and find a higher solution. We must make tough decisions that may impact the bottom line but will establish a new level of health for ourselves and our planet.

Chapter 20

A Basic Human Right is to Choose What is Right for Us

Your body's ability to heal is greater than anyone permitted you to believe.
Hazel Chandler

Photo by M Jennifer Chandler

In the Declaration of Independence we find the following statement. "We hold these truths to be self-evident, that all men are created equal, that they are endowed by their Creator with certain unalienable rights that among these are Life, Liberty and the pursuit of Happiness." I believe that at the roots of our country, we were given the unalienable right to choose. I believe that we are being asked to choose to live in the flow of life, celebrating our connection with each other. Many things have happened in the past 240 years that have disconnected our interaction with each other from these unalienable rights given to us in the Declaration of Independence.

When we are faced with cancer we are faced with a choice of how we walk the journey. Will we embrace the fear, give our power to the medical community, and use highly toxic chemicals to treat the condition that greatly impact our ability to live life to the fullest and pursue happiness? Or do we embrace love and make the choice to face our fears, stand in our power and take responsibility for all choices that we make? Embracing love does not necessarily reject the medical community and advances that have been made in the treatment, but it give us an opportunity to choose what the best road is for each of us to be able to heal.

For those of us that choose to walk another path to healing it is enticing to pick up on easy answers and think that we will have a quick recovery. Facebook is full of quick solutions and fast cures for cancer. One of the most prevalent is the baking soda cure. According to the articles, all a person needs to do is take baking soda to restore an alkaline environment and the cancer will go away. Extremes and both sides of the medical and natural medicine spectrum can be highly problematic.

For me, the choices that I made included a whole spectrum of solutions and options. Staying in the moment, connecting with my body and the earth were extremely important in informing these choices. Also choosing the right partners to assist with the journey was critical. For me the most important partner was my Naturopathic Medical Doctor.

Naturopathic Medical Doctors (NMD)

While not recognized as a primary care doctor by most insurances and not even licensed in every state, Naturopathic Medical Doctors are the perfect partner if your choice is to take an active role in your own healing process to address cancer. Naturopathic Medicine is a type of medicine that combines the healing power of nature with the traditional knowledge and prescribing rights of medical doctors.

My NMD recognizes the interconnection and interdependence of all living things, and together we created a plan to use the most natural, least invasive and least toxic therapies to treat cancer and promote wellness through viewing the body as an integrated whole. She became my partner in honoring my body's innate wisdom to heal. Her approach is based on six fundamental principle of Naturopathic Medicine. I think looking at these principles is important to understanding the importance of having a Naturopathic Physician as a partner in the healing process. They are:

The Healing Power of Nature
Trust in the body's inherent wisdom to heal itself.

Identify and Treat the Causes
Look beyond the symptoms to the underlying cause.

First Do No Harm
Utilize the most natural, least invasive and least toxic therapies.

Doctor as Teacher
Educate patients in the steps to achieving and maintaining health.

Treat the Whole Person
View the body as an integrated whole in all its physical and spiritual dimensions.

Prevention
Focus on overall health, wellness and disease prevention.

My partnership with my NMD created a plan to build my immune system that would allow my body's innate healing abilities to be unleashed. This included nutrition, supplements, exercise and life style changes as well as IV treatment designed to build the immune systems while also using natural ingredients known to have anti-cancer effects. In fact this is a natural non-toxic form of chemo, but with absolutely no side effects. While the focus was on restoring the alkaline environment to the body, the interrelated combination of treatment and life style changes were designed to stop inflammation in the body and restore balance.

It is with great sadness that I realize that everyone does not have the opportunity that I have to share the cancer journey with a Naturopathic Doctor who has had great results in treating cancer. Currently only 17 states license naturopathic doctors in this country, even though the naturopathic medical doctor program is as rigorous as the current MD program that is licensed in every state. Currently licensure is available in Alaska, Arizona, California, Connecticut, Hawaii, Idaho, Kansas, Maine, Minnesota, Montana, New Hampshire, North Dakota, Oregon, Utah, Vermont, Washington, plus the District of Columbia and the United States Territories, Puerto Rico and the Virgin Islands. Although legislation is being considered in a number of states, federal recognition will probably be required to allow everyone to have a choice of a Naturopathic Medical Doctor.

Currently only a handful of insurance companies recognize Naturopathic Medical Doctors and pay for the services provided. I was one of the lucky ones for a few months to have United Health Care that did pay for part of my treatment. But even then it was considered out of network and therefore had much higher deductible and co-pays. Since my retirement my medical insurance is now under Medicare. No matter the cost effectiveness of the treatment that I have chosen, they will not pay a single penny for my care. Together we must stand and demand our elected officials honor our right to choose our health partners. We need to demand choices beyond pill pushers in walking our journey towards healing.

In choosing a Naturopathic Doctor to assist with healing cancer it is very important to ask questions. What is this doctor's experience in treating cancer and what are the outcomes of the treatments provided? Does he/she have research on the effectiveness of the treatments? Does the NMD participate in an Internal Review Board to oversee the research aspects of the treatment provided? This provides another level of safety that the treatments that you are receiving are peer reviewed under the standard established by the National Institute of Health for human subject research.

Chiropractic Care

Chiropractors use hands-on spinal manipulation and other alternative treatments to align the body's musculoskeletal structure. The theory being that proper alignment of the body's musculoskeletal structure, particularly the spine, allows the body to heal itself. For me, my Chiropractor was critical in keeping the energy flowing through the body to allow the healing to occur. I tended to carry stress in my upper body, shoulders and neck, resulting in pain especially when I am using a computer, driving and other tasks. It was really easy for my imagination to go wild that the pain was from the cancer.

A quick trip to see Dr. Warner, my Chiropractor, would result in a reminder that the pain was from the tension and repetitive motion, not the cancer. Again I encourage you to carefully choose your treatment team. My Chiropractor uses a combination of massage and gentle adjustment to align my body. Many Chiropractors use only what I call crack and pop – a more aggressive form of adjustment which does not work well with my body. I still get a little crack and pop, but just a little more gentle. I would also be really suspicious of a Chiropractor that keeps you locked into coming a couple times a week for months. In my experience the best practitioners can restore alignment in a couple of appointments and then you will just require a tune-up after that initial treatment. My chiropractor laughs at me because I seem to come in for a tune-up (oil change) about every three months. We joke that it is time for an oil change.

Chiropractic care is often supported by traditional insurance and can be an important tool in treatment of cancer.

Energy Healing/Massage

Science is now telling us that our bodies are not solid as we have been taught to believe but energy- ever flowing. For me it seems like disease represents places in the body where the energy is not flowing smoothly. In fact, I feel there a connection between tumors in our body and this lack of energy flow in the area that does not allow the tissue to receive adequate oxygen. We know that cancer cannot survive in an oxygen-rich environment. Could the energy blocks in the body also cut off the oxygen to the cells in this area of the body? I think there may be a connection.

Massage therapy, energy healing, Reiki and other practices which move energy are important in the healing process. Again choose carefully. Pay attention to what your body is saying about the practitioner. Be particular about who works on your body. Some people's personal energy is so low that they take energy from you. Choose carefully. You will know in your gut whether this is a good choice.

Acupuncture

Acupuncture originated in China over 2,000 years ago. It is a procedure that involves stimulation of anatomical points in the body using a variety of techniques, but usually involves the use of needles. This traditional medical tradition originating from China, Japan, Korea and other countries has been shown to be helpful with many diseases and is helpful to release energy blocks in the body and relieve pain caused by cancer. Again some insurance companies will support acupuncture. It may be worth checking out, especially as a way to address pain.

Nutrition

My Naturopath provided me a nutritional plan to follow. It was really simple. Lots of fruits and vegetables, nuts, legumes, small amount of organic meats, good fats (olive oil, nuts, coconut oil) and limited whole grains such as quinoa and other ancient gains. I was to eliminate all sugar, processed foods, alcohol, flours, trans-fats, etc. I had extensively studied nutrition and was able to stick to the eating plan without a problem.

A nutritionist could be a good resource, but in my experience few really understand eating to cure cancer. I will be providing support, ideas and recipes on my website www.beyondthebigc. com and at the Beyond the Big C Facebook page. You can sign up on both pages for newsletters and blogs that will support healthy eating.

Exercise

For me exercise has been key in my healing process. I encourage you to find an exercise program that works for you. It might be a variety of things. Walking is probably the easiest, and it is free. I also love to climb a local mountain. I use Curves to support strength training and endurance, which allows me the freedom to work at my own pace. I think research is showing that gentle exercise is as good/or possibly even better than aggressive exercise. The key is regular exercise. Early in my cancer journey the exercise was gentle. I am now exercising with much more vigor and stamina. Listen to your body and what it needs.

Control Your Toxic Load

We live in a very toxic world. No matter how hard we try, we are confronted by toxins that are potential carcinogens. We get toxins with every breath, every bite of food and drop of water that we drink. It has been said that the average person puts an average of 200 potential toxins on or in our body before we even leave our house in the morning. It is extremely important to educate yourself on the products that you use, and the potential chemicals in household products, and on the food that you eat. None of us can avoid coming in contact with toxins, but we can make good informed choices that assist with controlling the toxic load.

One of the first choices is to buy organic whenever possible. Next we need to address the cleaning products and body care products that we use in our home. Just because a product is sold at a health food store does not mean that it is free of toxic substances. Educate yourself about your household products and toxins in your personal care items and household cleaning supplies. Even though toxic-free choices are currently limited, every time we purchase an organic, toxic-free product we are voting with our pocketbook. Businesses are listening, and we are beginning to see healthier options.

Another choice could be a natural product in our kitchen that works as a great substitute. Vinegar and baking soda work great for cleaning. Baking soda and coconut oil make a great toothpaste. Again check out the website and Facebook pages for more information.

This is just the tip of the iceberg of the choices that we have to support our journey. Remember that all healing starts inside, and we must heal inside out.

Chapter 21

Healing our Planet and Ourselves Through Changing the Way We Look at Life

Progress is impossible without change, and those who cannot change their minds cannot change anything.

George Bernard Shaw

As I have walked the spiritual journey towards my own healing, I have come to realize that we are the earth we live on and that disease in the body is a reflection of greater imbalances in the biosphere that we call Planet Earth. Our planet is a big blue marble, really a space ship hurling through the solar system every day. The earth is above us, below us, around us and in us. Just like our earth is part of the greater solar system and universe, we are part of the body we call planet earth. In fact each of us are really cells in that body. Everything that we call 'us' is made of the earth. The water, our bones and the microscopic cells in our bodies are part of the earth. In fact science has confirmed without a doubt that Earth is truly an alive living being. Understanding this gives us an opportunity to transform our relationship with our bodies and our planet.

A few hundred years ago the belief of many was the world was flat and that the sun, moon and star revolved around us. In more recent years we have developed a belief that the earth is an inanimate object that we can rape and pillage at will to support our needs. Our economic and political systems, in fact our way of life, have been based on this belief. When the population of the earth was small and the needs of the population were simple, the earth was able to meet those needs without a major threat to its health and well-being. Today we have 7 billion 402 million people on this planet, and this is increasing every second. A month and a half into 2016 we have increased the world population by over 10 million. This is up from a total world population of less than a half of a billion in the mid 1600s. Our demands for resources to support our way of life have greatly exceeded the ability of the planet to sustain life. We are seeing breakdown all around us that shows we have greatly exceeded the carrying capacity of our planet. The cancer epidemic is just one of those signs.

For over 30 years I have been extremely concerned about issues facing our planet such as climate change, environmental issues and other indications that our biosphere is unraveling. The science that I studied in the 80s made predictions of what could happen with climate change if we did not change our ways. These predictions for what would happen in 2050 or 2100 missed the mark and not in a good way. In the 80s I was concerned about my grandchildren and great grandchildren. Those predictions that were made in the 80s are happening right now 35 to 75 years early. I never dreamed that I should be concerned about my future as well. We have lost thirty-five years mired in the denial, living in a worldview that we are separate from the earth and each other. We have bought into a worldview of fear, anger, and prejudices of 'I win you lose.' We have bought into the worldview that the planet is an inanimate object for us to rape and pillage. A worldview that we can spew more toxins into our biosphere and our bodies without concern about the long-terms effects just to make another product that will soon end up in the ocean or a landfill. The impacts of this worldview are catching up with us. Cancer is just one of the manifestation of this toxic soup that we have created.

What if we changed that worldview to realize that we are all on this earth together and each of us is a living cell in the greater body of our planet? What if we looked at each other with love and realized that we are all interconnected?

Just like cancer was a wake-up call for me to find healing within, it has been a huge wake-up call for me that we need to pay attention to our mother planet earth and all of Earth's inhabitants. The issues facing our planet today cannot be healed with the same worldview that created these problems, just like we cannot cure cancer with the same worldview.

Time has come for all of us to join together and say enough is enough. We will not allow business and our governments to separate us and keep us locked in an endless cycle of fear, anger and separateness. We will not allow a few powerful businessmen to buy our elections and continue to create a toxic soup that threatens our basic survival and that of every living thing on earth. We will come together as a community from a place of personal power, love and commitment to heal ourselves and our planet. We will find solutions to a myriad of life-threatening issues that we are facing. Together we will choose life and choose public policy that enhances life for all inhabitants of this planet. Through love we will find the cure for cancer.

Eckert Tolle says that healing requires a change in our level of consciousness. Being more present is a key to changes at a conscious level. "Negativity is totally unnatural. It is a psychic pollutant and there is a deep link between the poisoning and destruction of nature and the vast negativity that has accumulated in the collective human psyche. No other life form on planet knows negativity, only humans, just as no other life forms violates and poisons the earth that sustains it." *Eckert Tolle "Power of Now"*

Can we move beyond our fear and negativity and create a future of a vibrantly healthy planet and vibrant health for all its inhabitants? I think so.

Chapter 22

Celebrating our Grand Diversity

We are each and all cells in the body of an evolving giant super-organism we call humanity. Because humans have free will, we can choose to either rise to that new level of emergence or, in the manner of dinosaurs, fall by the wayside.

Bruce Lipton

Like it or not, our future depends on the choices we make as a species.

Amerca is the greatest experiment of all times. Nowhere anywhere in the world do we see such diversity of race, religion, sexual orientation and country of origin living side by side. We have been living in our cities with people from virtually every country in the world, many countries that most of us would not be able to find on the map.

As we look around we see this grand diversity everywhere, not just in segregated neighborhoods. In my condos alone we have families easily from at least 60 countries that have recently immigrated to our country. If we look at the generational backgrounds of people living here that number would easily double. Here in America we live side by side in relative peace. Our children are growing up with a rainbow of playmates from diverse ethnic and religious backgrounds. To our children this is normal and definitely not something to be concerned about.

Here in America we have a grand opportunity to be a role model for the world. The time has come for the diverse America to come together to honor our diversity and understand that we are really all the same. We have the same basic needs to love, be loved and to make a difference with our lives.

Although there are some differences in the way we look at life that stem from our ethnic and religious backgrounds, the basis of these beliefs have many similarities. When we can really listen to people of diverse backgrounds we form a common ground on which to base a friendship. This common ground also allows us to look at issues through the eyes of others and better understand their point of view.

The time has come when we must embrace our diversity and breakdown the barriers of fear that has such a stronghold on our country. As we can truly embrace our own national diversity, we can serve as role models for the rest of the world. We can open dialogues around the world to restore the image of the U.S. in the world community as well as serve as a role model to ending ethic and racial tensions all over the world.

I believe that the diseases that are affecting so many of us are huge wakeup calls. Cancer affects everyone, across all races and belief systems. Earth is right now in a huge state of transformation that we have the opportunity to flow with or leave just before the final inning.

I believe we are not only being asked to heal our bodies through loving ourselves, but to heal our relationship with life. To **LOVE** more!!!

We are being asked to heal how we interact with life. Medicine can assist some people in winning the war against cancer, but does not heal the underlying causal relationships that allow the cancer in the first place. I believe that we are being asked to examine our own belief systems. To reevaluate what is real and what is not. All around us we see breakdown. Breakdown is seen out-pictured as war, poverty, violence in the street, child abuse, domestic violence, and a disease care system that does not work. Schools that do not give children the tools that they need to live a 21st century life. An economic system that rewards the top 1% and leaves the rest behind. I do not believe this reflects who we truly are.

I believe today is the day that we can move beyond the control that disease has on us by healing the core issues that have allowed disease to get a foothold in our body and through this healing we can live a Vibrantly Healthy life.

Do you choose to live life or die life? Are you going to be a catalyst for the transformation of the planet, or are you going to sit idly by and watch our planet's cancer/AIDS continue to grow, taking away the life force of all life? The choice is yours.

Each of you has a unique role to play in the healing process. Are you choosing Vibrant Life??? I hope so – I want to explore ways that we can play together. Drink another Vegetable Juice and celebrate this Vibrant Health with me. Love everyone around you – no exceptions – and dance to the music of the universe.

Remember the Keys to Health

- ❑ Hydration
- ❑ Absorption/Assimilation
- ❑ Adequate Nutrition
- ❑ Exercise – Movement of Body Energy
- ❑ Mental and Emotional Thoughts – Clarity
- ❑ Desire/Purpose for Life
- ❑ Live Life in Joy, Play, Fun, Laughter, Love

Naturopathic Cancer Society

Author's notes: I am excited to donate a portion of the proceeds of this book to a new type of cancer charity that really helps people living with cancer. Each of us deserves a choice in our care, but many cannot afford the choices that they make.

With recent media attention on the federal government going after some of the largest cancer charities, it is time to re-evaluate how best to support people with cancer and get funding to the people who need help the most. The public is fed up with the mainstream cancer charities that play on our emotions, but little of the money raised gets to the people that need it. Naturopathic Cancer Society is unique among cancer charities in that **85 cents of every dollar donated** goes directly to provide treatment for people living with cancer.

As this book has outlined, current standards of care for cancer, such as chemotherapy and radiation, poison the body, deplete vitality and greatly impact "Quality of Life" often for years after the treatments have been completed. Naturopathic treatment has been shown to provide an effective option that builds the immune system and greatly enhances the quality of life.

Traditional cancer charities receive billions in donations every year, but only a small fraction of the funds actually provide treatments. Most of their revenue goes to fundraising, overhead and pharmaceutical research devoted to the same toxic approaches to treatment. With billions invested in cancer charities, we are not any closer to fully understanding and curing cancer than we were 40 years ago when we first declared war on cancer.

Many people are asking: Is there a better way? A better way to treat cancer as well as a better way to support people living with cancer. Naturopathic Cancer Society embraces a better way on both fronts. First people living with cancer get financial support to receive naturopathic treatments that have been proven to allow people to heal from cancer while maintaining vitality and quality of life. 85 cents of every dollar donated fund direct grants to allow people living with cancer to get Naturopathic treatment. Naturopathic cancer treatment has some of the top cancer success rates in the world at a fraction of the cost of traditional cancer treatment.

Secondly, Naturopathic Cancer Society is building a unique non-profit model for the future based on people helping people. Naturopathic Cancer Society is committed to fully embrace volunteerism, social media and word of mouth fundraising to allow people to have a choice in the treatment that they choose in response to cancer. Low and moderate income individuals needing assistance to afford Naturopathic treatment options must commit to living a healthy lifestyle. Naturopathic Cancer Society believes that giving and receiving is part of the healing process. Grant recipients are encouaged to find their unique way to pay forward the support given. This can be service to others living with cancer, testimonials, fund raising, monetary donations. Each person is encouraged to follow their passion on how to serve.

People living with Cancer deserve a choice. Whether they choose to combine naturopathic treatment with conventional treatment or to use Naturopathic as the only treatment, patients deserve to be able to choose what is best for them without financial constraints.

Thank you for giving life to a person facing cancer through supporting my book. A portion of every book sales will be donated to Naturopathic Cancer Society.

If you would like to rethink societies approach to Cancer and give knowing where your donations are going, I encourage you to give more at www.natonco.org. The Naturopathic Cancer Society is the answer, and all donors giving $2,000 or more will receive a summary of people helped by their donation and can get to know the stories of people that they are helping. For more information: www.natonco.org

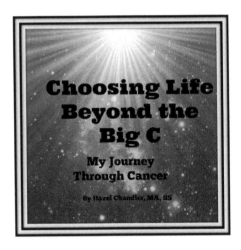

Beyond the Big C, LLC

www.beyondthebigC.com

hazelchandler@beyondthebigC.com

Join us at Beyond the Big C website for information on my journey to healing, tips on creating perfect health and resources that enhance that journey.

Nature Works Best

C A N C E R   C L I N I C

My Treatment Team

Dr. Colleen Huber and Staff

www.natureworksbest.com
480-839-2800

Not just Any Natural Cancer Clinic

Nature Works Best is a natural cancer clinic located in Tempe, Arizona that focuses on natural, holistic, and naturopathic treatments of cancer. They do not use chemotherapy or radiation in their treatments. Rather, they have developed a unique method of treating cancer based on intravenous vitamin therapy as well as a simple food plan.

The team of naturopathic medical doctors has administered over 15,000 intravenous treatments, used for all stages and types of cancer with amazing success. That is, 83% of patients who complete the treatments alone go into remission, 90% of patients who complete their treatments and follow their food plan go into remission; no other clinic, of any kind, has such a high documented success rate. The cancer patients come to them with different types of cancer, at different stages, often with different co-morbidities, and different patterns of metastases.

They have seen patients of all stages of cancer do very well with their treatments, with the exception of late stage IV patients. As of July 2013, 317 cancer patients have come to the clinic in Stages

1, 2, 3 or 4. Yet they have only lost 32 patients to cancer in the last five years of using the protocols. Another 20 died from either chemotherapy or other hospital experiences. All of the latter were late stage cancer patients who had already been severely sickened by their conventional cancer treatments, some even coming out of hospice for the treatments.

Naturopathic Cancer Research

Cancer research has been almost exclusively focused on pharmaceutical research. Research is an expensive endeavor, and up until now only products that can receive a patent have been recipients of most of the research focus. In 2010 a group of Naturopathic Doctors formed the American Naturopathic Research Institute (ANRI) and an Internal Review Board (IRB) to explore and to conduct research on causes and treatments for chronic disease including but not limited to cancer, diseases of inflammation and disordered immune function and environmentally-caused illness.

The group also came together to preserve naturopathic medicine as practiced in all the diversity, synergy and comprehensiveness as it presently exists in the states with the broadest scope of practice, as well as to create the possibility of growth in ideas, research and treatment opportunities in order to further expand the knowledge and capabilities of the profession.

Out of that original effort, "The Naturopathic Oncology Research Institute (NORI)" and the IRB have been formed in order to explore and to conduct research on treatments related to cancer, its causes and manifestations while striving for the greatest possible treatment choice, wellbeing, strengthening, education and empowerment of patients with cancer. The group's focus is as follows:

- Provide a forum of peers as well as public members dedicated to embracing the breadth of naturopathic medicine, including its many diverse practice modalities in a non-judgmental way.
- Re-affirm the standards of care in naturopathic medicine being based on the greater good of our patients' need for the optimal treatment strategy for their health circumstances and that this best treatment protocol for any given patient is most likely to be found among a very broad scope of practice rather than one that is unnecessarily restricted.
- Recognize that two or more individual practitioners in the naturopathic community practicing in a particular way with regard to patient care, or as taught in a naturopathic school of medicine, are generally considered as adequate by Naturopathic Board of Medicine to establish such treatments as valid for ongoing study and practice.

Out of the beginning the group has grown to over thirty Phoenix area Naturopathic Physicians as well participation by a number of other physicians in other states as well as other countries. The Internal Review Board is recognized by the National Institute of Health under the laws of conducting human subject research.

This board is current overseeing a number of research protocols that have shown to be very effective in the treatment of cancer and other environmental and immune diseases. While it is impossible to conduct double blind studies, the safety and effectiveness of the treatment protocols are evaluated with much rigor from the review board, which consists of a group of their peers. These protocols allow sharing successful treatments and collaborative collection of data that build the knowledge base about using these natural and non-toxic treatments to support people restore their health.

I have been privileged to serve as a patient representative on the Investigational Review Board for over two years, and I can attest that it is every bit as rigorous as the Boards that I participated in while training with the National Institute of Health. It is refreshing to me to hear the Review Board talk about enhancing a person's life and well-being, not just how we can mitigate the side effects of the pharmaceutical or even worse with chemo products how close to death can we take the patients that I have experienced on the more traditional IRBs. I have learned a tremendous amount from these quarterly meetings, and each time I walk out of a meeting I realize that we have the tools to make the Cancer Moonshot a success. When we use the expertise of all medical providers we open the doors to a new level of innovation and find new ways of approaching disease. It is a real privilege to serve on this IRB. For more information check out Andri/Nori's web-site.

http://naturopathicstandards.org/

Resources to Check Out

Alternative Treatment Resources - Books

Blaylock, Russell L., MD, Natural Strategies for Cancer Patients, Kensington Publishing Corp, New York, 2003, www.kensington-books.com

Fuhrman, Joel, MD, *Eat to Live*, Little Brown and Company, New York, 2011

Huber, Colleen, MND, *Choose your Foods – Like your Life Depends on Them*, Xlibris Corporation, 2007, www.Xlibris.com

Siegel, Bernie, MD, *How to Live Between Office Visits – A Guide to Life, Love and Health, Harper Collins Publishers, New York, 2001*

Somers, Suzanne, *Knockout – Interviews with Doctors that Are Curing Cancer-*Three Rivers Press, New York, 2009

Strasheim, Connie, *Defeat Cancer*, Biomed Publishing Group, South Lake Tahoe, CA, 2011 – www.BioMedPublishers.com

Some of My Favorite Books

Chopra, Deepak, Ford, Debbie, Williamson, Marianne, *The Shadow Effect Illuminating the Hidden Power of Your True Self*, Harper One, New York, 2010

Dyer, Dr. Wayne W., *Inspiration Your Ultimate Calling*, Hay House, 2006

Ford, Debbie, *The Secret of the Shadow*, Harper San Francisco, 2002

Ford, Debbie, *Courage-Overcoming Fear and Igniting Self Confidence*, Harper One, New York, 2012

Goldsmith, Joel, *The Art of Spiritual Healing*, Harper, SanFrancisco, 1959

Hay, Louise, *You Can Heal Your Life*, Hay House, Santa Monica, CA, 1984

Lipton, Bruce, *The Biology of Belief*, Hay House 2008

Singer, Michael A, *The Untethered Soul-The Journey Beyond Yourself*, Oakland, CA: New Harbinger Publications. 2007

Tamura, Michael, *You are the Answer*, Llewellyn Publications, Woodbury, MN, 2013

Tolle, Eckhart, *A New Earth – Awakening to Your Life's Purpose*, Penguin Group, New York, 2005

Tolle, Eckhart, *The Power of Now – A Guide to Spiritual Enlightment, New World Library, Navato, CA, 1999* Penguin Group, New York, 2005

Williamson, Marianne, *The Gift of Change – Spiritual Guidance for a Radically New Life*, Harper San Francisco, 2004

Zukav, Gary, *Spiritual Partnership – The Journey to Authentic Power*, Harper One, New York, 2010, www.seatofthesoul.com

Zukav, Gary, *Seat of the Soul*, Gary Zukav, www.seatofthesoul.com

Zukav, Gary, *The Mind of the Soul – Responsible Choice*, Free Press, New York, 2003 www.seatofthesoul.com

Biography for Hazel Chandler

 My life journey has led me on many paths in life. Unlike my father who worked the same job for years, I was led in many directions. For the last 50 years of my adult life I have had many adventures and played many roles in government, private for profit and non-profit organizations. My broad based management experience includes health care, social services, mental health, early childhood education, primary education, government, regulatory environment, construction, development, retail business, small business ownership, international business, community planning, investments and financial management.

My life dedicated to service has led me to work with people of all ages, from every walk of life, ethnic and cultural backgrounds. Through all of the twists and turns of life I had extensive opportunities to look at the systems that support our life in America and realized that most were not working to enhance life. Through the years I have studied extensively preventive and alternative health care, education, environmental issues, self-development, mind-body-spirit healing and nutrition.

Through all of these experiences I had many opportunities to work with Federal, State and Local Governments.

My Bachelor's Degree and Graduate work is in Early Childhood Development from San Diego State University, with minors in education, sociology and psychology. In the early 80s, after marriage and children, I went on to receive a Master's degree in Management from University of Phoenix. In June of 2012 I completed the Arizona State University program and obtained the Certified Public Manager Certification.